EMOTIONAL WOUND First Aid Kit

A Comprehensive Workbook for Healing
and Optimal Emotional Health & Wellness

John Schurmann M.S.W., R.S.W.

Publisher's Note

This publication is designed to provide accurate and authoritative information in regard to the subject matter covered. It is sold with the understanding that the publisher is not engaged in rendering psychological, financial, legal, or other professional services. If expert assistance or counseling is needed, the services of a competent professional should be sought.

The content of this workbook is the author's opinion only, and is to be used by the reader at his/her own will.

No other warranty is given for using the content of the workbook.

Confidentiality is essential to therapeutic practice. All case descriptions in this book, therefore, have been altered to preserve the anonymity of my clients without distorting the essentials of their stories.

The information offered in this workbook is not intended to be a substitute for the advice and counsel of your personal therapist, life coach or physician.

I dedicate this work to those of you who are feeling emotionally wounded, stuck, alone, hurting, despairing and looking to build courage to face your emotional wounds, commit to doing the healing work, change in ways you never imagined possible and grow into the whole person you are capable of being.

Table of Contents

Acknowledgement

I'd like to first thank God for giving me the creativity, strength and grace to write on healing and optimal emotional health & wellness. Without Your inspiration the Emotional Wound First Aid Kit would not have been crafted.

Special thanks go to my psychology professors: Dr. Brian Johnson, Dr. Jim Geddes, and Dr. Harold Faw at Trinity Western University. Your theorizing, meticulous research, and teachings have stimulated my own thinking on emotional healing immeasurably.

I express gratitude to the theorists and practitioners who influenced my writing. John & Paula Standford wrote The Transformation of the Inner Man. Francis MacNutt (Healing) and (The Power to Heal). Rita Bennett (Making Peace With Your Inner Child) and David A Seamands (Healing of Memories).

A very special thanks to my clients, some older, some younger, for sharing your healing stories. Plus, you have helped me sharpen the theory and practice of teaching emotional wound care. You are the most courageous people I have ever met. I will always be grateful for your heroism – achieving full and lasting emotional recovery.

Thanks to Virginia Gedge, Rita Schurmann and Emily Cox for the care and attention you gave to the editing of this workbook, for your flexibility and patience in helping me organize my thoughts and ideas in a way that would make sense to you.

Finally, I wish to acknowledge my sincere gratitude to my wife. You stood by me even when I had not yet learned the lessons that are laid out in this First Aid Kit. You are my love and inspiration.

Introduction

With the potential to change millions of lives, the Emotional Wound First-Aid Kit can truly change your life. I am convinced that it will be read, reread, and recommended as an essential tool. Physicians, therapists, patients, and all those seeking to heal their emotional wounds and develop optimal emotional health & wellness can benefit greatly from it.

When I first began using the program in my private practice, I had no idea that it would become one of the most successful and effective tools to help heal emotional injuries, emotional wounds and emotional pain. It is now a vital part of my treatment model.

The strategies described in this Emotional Wound First Aid Kit can help you solve your intimacy, shame, guilt, anger, loss, relationship, depression, anxiety and addiction issues, and improve your self-esteem. It can help you restore and enhance your emotional, intellectual and spiritual health. It also teaches techniques that have been helpful with emotional injuries such as sexual abuse, violence and psychological trauma. Furthermore, the program will provide the central self-care skills to help you develop a healthy, vibrant and resilient mind, heart and spirit. And, it can help you learn to love and appreciate yourself passionately.

Many who have used the methods outlined in this workbook have come to view the initial discomfort that led them to the Emotional Wound First Aid Kit as a "blessing in disguise." Through their pain, they have discovered this step-by-step first aid program based on sound principles to help restore and maintain emotional health. I trust this will be your experience too!

The approach teaches you to apply and practice the skills until they become second nature. Having the knowledge alone is not enough. Each step in the program is based on mastery of the work that precedes it. However painful the steps may be, they are necessary, to begin the path to healing. Do not read through this book quickly. Instead, commit now to applying and mastering each step before moving on to the next one. Give yourself sufficient time to complete each step. Although the steps may look easy at first glance, once you start the work, they can be more complex and difficult than they seem.

How this First Aid Kit is organized

This first aid kit consists of **seven steps**:

1. Cleaning Your Wound
2. Destroying the Contaminants
3. Treating Your Wound
4. Protecting Your Wound
5. Nurturing Your Emotions
6. Loving Your Inner-Child
7. Loving God

We will examine the reasons for, the importance of, and the ways of successfully completing each of these critical steps. Powerful case studies are provided to helpful illustrate the implementation of this process.

Facts about Emotional Wound Care

What does emotional pain feel like or look like? How do you assess the seriousness of an emotional injury, wound or pain? What are the normal responses to emotional trauma? We are usually well informed about the symptoms and treatment procedures for physical injury. We expect the injury to hurt and heal.

Regarding emotional injury and bruising, however, we are not sure what to expect. Most people think they know all the facts when it comes to the topic of emotional wound care – "if someone hurts or bruises my emotions, I'll just cover them up and I'm ready to go!" Unfortunately, it is not as simple as that. An emotional wound needs the same special treatment as a physical injury, in order to heal most efficiently and minimize the appearance of scars.

So, before you cover up the hurt or injury, you need to know the difference between the facts and the misconceptions on emotional wound care.

Misconception: An emotional wound heals best when left alone. Time will do the trick.

Fact: Leaving an emotional wound alone actually slows down the healing process and can lead to further emotional infection and distasteful scars. Increased emotional discomfort and pain often produce symptoms such as anger, stress, fatigue, sadness, irritability, moodiness, resentment, bitterness, loneliness, jealousy and insecurity, just to mention a few.

Untreated emotional wounds can cause physical, mental, emotional and spiritual problems. They can set off mental health disorders such as depression, anxiety and addiction. These wounds can wipe out relationships, lead to job failures, obscure life's purpose or direction, and ultimately destroy life.

Misconception: It is best to let an emotional wound "air out".

Fact: "Talking it out" or "journaling" is the first step in handling an emotional wound. This technique used by itself, without full treatment is, however, as harmful as leaving it alone. Always talking about your pain will not heal the wound. Although you may experience a momentary degree of release, your wound will worsen over time.

Misconception: "Getting even" with the other person is the best way to deal with any emotional injury.

Fact: Getting even with the person who caused the injury may, for a while, release a degree of emotional pain. But in the long run, this action will further inflame your wound. A negative reaction or strategy will create further self-injury. This will only further inflict your wound and make matters worse.

Emotional Wound Assessment Tool

To find out if you have emotional injuries, wounds and pains, complete the following Emotional Wound Assessment Tool:

Exercise: Circle the numbers of the statements that apply to you.

1. I often suppress my feelings.

2. I feel hurt at times, but cannot understand why.

3. People say that I seldom or never show my emotions.

4. Most people do not understand my emotions.

5. I avoid thoughts, feelings or conversations about a hurtful event in my life.

6. I am unhappy and sad most of the time.

7. I often choose to keep a hurtful event a secret.

8. I find it difficult to show sensitivity toward others.

9. I do not get close to people and/or I feel "on guard".

10. I avoid activities, places or people who remind me of a hurtful event in my life.

11. I hold anger toward some people.

12. I do not forgive people who have wronged me.

13. I have difficulty-trusting people.

14. I can hold a grudge for a long time.

15. I am critical of myself and of other people.

16. I sense that my future is short/limited *(e.g. I don't expect to have a career, marriage, children, or a normal life span).*

17. I am more irritable and have outbursts of anger.

18. I have difficulty sleeping and/or I cry a lot.

19. I am afraid to confront people who have hurt me.

20. I feel my range of emotions is restricted.

21. I lost interest in significant activities in my life.

22. I self-medicate with alcohol, drugs, sex or work.

23. I have physical and/or emotional distress when I am exposed to things that remind me of a hurtful event in my life.

24. I have repeated, distressing memories and/or dreams.

25. I have been hurt a month ago or longer and I have not dealt with it.

26. I feel guilty and/or shamed.

27. I let people take advantage of me.

28. I am still grieving a loss after so many years.

29. I have never let go of betrayal, loss or hurt.

30. I have experienced or witnessed a life-threatening event two months ago, and it still causes intense fear, helplessness or horror.

Scoring Key for the Emotional Pain Scale

Total Score	Degree of Pain
0-4	Minimal or no pain
5-10	Moderate pain
11-20	Severe pain
21-30	Extreme pain

Note: If more than five statements are circled there is reason to suspect that an emotional injury, wound or pain is present in your life. The First Aid Kit comes with tools to help you heal your wounds, maintain healthy emotions, and foster a healthy mind, heart and spirit.

Emotional Wounds

Healing an emotional injury, wound or pain is much like healing a physical wound. Left untreated, a wound or open sore can cause serious problems.

Living with an untreated wound can yield feelings of anger, irritability, moodiness and hopelessness. It can cause mental health disorders such as depression, anxiety, phobia and addictions. Left untreated, such a wound can contaminate every aspect of your life. Open wounds affect how you view the world, how you relate to others and how you conduct your life in general. Emotional wounds must be restored before you will feel whole again.

Although a wide range of life factors can bring about an emotional injury, wound and pain, most are caused by:

1. Yourself or other people that emotionally hurt.
2. Life events that emotionally hurt.

Feelings such as anger, anxiety, stress, depression, hurt, guilt, shame, frustration, emptiness and loneliness are side effects of self-wounding caused by our own beliefs, thoughts and actions. Painful feelings such as aloneness, heartache and heartbreak, helplessness over others, grief, sorrow over people hurting other people, sorrow over people hurting us or outrage over injustice are a result of life.

Definition

An emotional wound is the result of an emotional injury inflicted by self, by another person or life events that have not yet healed.

It is estimated that 15 to 20 percent of people who seek professional counseling for depression or anxiety have at the root of the symptoms unresolved grief/trauma. These can result from events ranging from the death of a child or parent, to abuse, amputation, accidents, crime, or job loss (Worden 1982). Symptoms can include emotional numbing, depression, physical stress symptoms, anxiety, panic attacks and anger.

Emotional Wounds Caused by Yourself or a Person

- Saying and doing things to hurt yourself or a person.
- Rude, degrading or offensive remarks toward self or a person.
- Gestures that seek to intimidate and control self or a person.
- Discrediting yourself or a person by spreading rumors.
- Lying, cheating or using the person.
- Belittling, disregarding, devaluing, disrespecting yourself or a person.
- Preventing yourself or a person from expressing oneself.
- Yelling, threatening, prohibiting yourself or someone from speaking.
- Isolating self or a person - no longer talking to yourself or to another person, denying yourself or another person's presence, distancing yourself or a person from others.
- Invalidating, ridiculing, humiliating, shouting abuse toward self or a person.
- Self-inflicted offences brought on by you such as drugs, alcohol, sexual, gambling and Internet addiction.
- Inflicting physical, emotional and sexual abuse on yourself or a person.

Emotional Wounds Caused by Life Events

- Death of a loved one, friend or colleague.
- Ending of an important relationship (boyfriend/girlfriend).
- Marital separation, divorce and extra marital-affair.
- Broken family due to divorce, devastating event or war.
- Feelings of hurt - a child or friend moving away (or your moving away).
- Physical impairment – accident, illness, etc.
- Loss of a pet, property, or material possession.
- Feelings of hurt associated with moving away from school, neighbors, home, country, etc.
- Recognizing that dreams will not be realized.
- Witnessed or experienced a trauma, a devastating event, violence an assault, rape, war or persecution.
- Witness or experienced physical, emotional or sexual abuse.

A Mixture of Symptoms

An emotional injury, wound or pain releases a mixture of emotional, physical and cognitive symptoms, and a certain degree of pain.

Emotional Symptoms

Emotional mistreatments, injuries or traumas can cause emotional wounds. Injuries caused by you, a person or events create open sores or deep emotional wounds that release a mixture of unpleasant emotional and cognitive symptoms and a certain amount of hurt.

Some examples of unpleasant emotions are; anger, fear, loss, anxiety, sadness, despair, shame and guilt.

The degree of pain can range from: (1) minimal, to (10) severe on an emotional pain scale.

Depending on the severity of the emotional injury, the intensity of the blow can also cause invisible emotional bleeding and brokenness, such as a sudden ending of an important relationship - leaving the person heart broken.

Physical Symptoms

A long-lasting untreated emotional wound can also trigger physical symptoms such as: nerve disorders, allergies, stomach problems, heartaches, insomnia, headaches, stress, physical pains and unexplained physical illnesses.

Cognitive Symptoms

Emotional pain often triggers automatic negative thoughts (ANTs) and false beliefs. The negative thoughts or messages one gives oneself are often specific messages that are distorted like "I am a jerk," "You are such a looser!" and short messages "Stupid," or "Idiot". Distorted ANTs occur so fast that we hardly notice them. We repeat them to ourselves in our minds without thinking about them. And they are hard to turn off.

We usually end up believing them no matter how untrue they are. They may include assuming self-talk such as, "If I open up to my pain, I will fall into a pit," or "There is no point in talking about my pain." Others may believe that showing their feelings and pains is a sign of weakness, "Boys don't cry."

Degree of Emotional Pain

The size and depth of your emotional wound and the point in time in which it occurred, must also be evaluated. Did the emotional pain and injustice cause a large and deep wound or a small surface injury? When did the injury take place? The period of time between the injury and the disclosure is critical.

For instance, a sexual assault kept hidden for many years will potentially cause greater harm to a person's life than a recent exposed occurrence. Although in both cases the sexual assault produced the same amount of pain, immediate treatment of the injury will have less damaging after-effects than an untreated long-standing wound.

This process gives us a way of measuring the amount of pain and injustice the person has been exposed to. This evaluation is fairly subjective and therefore rather difficult to measure. To address this difficulty, I have divided the "degree of pain experienced" by the injury into two categories: (1) low-impact wound, and (2) high-impact wound.

Example of a Low-Impact Wound - an insult may trigger the following unpleasant emotional symptoms and irrational cognitive symptoms:

- **Mixture of feelings** - anger, hurt, fear, shame, guilt or indifference.
- **Degree of pain** – minimal to moderate.
- **Size of wound** – small.
- **Depth of wound** – surface injury.
- **Time period from the injury to disclosure**: 4 hours.
- **Physical Symptoms** – none.
- **Cognitive Symptoms** – "It was my fault and I deserve the insult."

A low-impact wound will generally elicit a minimal to moderate degree of pain and will typically heal in a short time. The interval between the incident and its disclosure is critical in minimizing the risk of further infection and maximizing the healing process. The sooner you talk about any emotional injury with a trusted person, the quicker your wound will heal.

Other examples of low-impact wounds are: an abusive shout, a lie, a rumor, an offensive remark or a humiliating experience. Since treating these wounds is less complex and time consuming than treating high-impact wounds, most people have the appropriate skills to resolve this type of injury.

Example of High-Impact Wound - sexual abuse may trigger the following unpleasant emotional, cognitive and physical symptoms:

- **Mixture of feelings** - hurt, anger, fear, confusion, loss, anxiety, sadness, depression, despair, loneliness, humiliation, betrayal, helplessness, shame, guilt, disgust, etc.

- **Size of wound** – multiple large wounds.

- **Depth of wound** – very deep.

- **Time from the injury to disclosure:** 30 years.

- **Degree of pain** – severe to extreme.

- **Physical Symptoms** - nerve disorders, stomach problems, insomnia, headaches, stress, unexplained physical illnesses, and physical pain – such as knee, shoulder, gums, etc.

- **Cognitive Symptoms** – "I have to be perfect because anything less is a failure. I'm a failure. If people knew the real me, they wouldn't like me. I'm flawed."

Sexual abuse, rape, violence, an extra-marital affair, severe physical and emotional abuse, and severe trauma are additional examples of high impact wounds.

A high-impact wound with deep, complex and long-standing emotional and cognitive sores will typically take a longer period of time, and greater patience and effort to heal. Furthermore, because of the multiple issues surrounding this type of wound, professional support is required to guide the healing process.

Unfortunately, most people use incorrect and inadequate tools to deal with their high-impact wounds. Instead of treating abuse with talk therapy, a person may try to soothe the bruise with food, alcohol or illegal drugs.

We all want to try to fix our wounds in our own ways. I applaud people who want to help themselves get better. Unfortunately, the laymen's tools are found to be inefficient and often destructive. How often are we coached by well-meaning friends to ignore the issues and not to confront an injustice?

We are told: "Don't bring it up because things could get even worse," or "If she ever finds out that you talked about this, you'll get fired".

In both personal and work environments, too often people fail to confront injustice, harassment, and abuse or control issues. Disregarding ill treatment due to fear of reprisal or loss of either an important job or relationship is wrong! It is as wrong as ignoring an open wound. Such action will promote further emotional harm and long term, possible life threatening, damage.

Take a moment and think about your last physical wound. How long did it take to heal? Did the wound heal? Not until you started attending to the wound by confronting the injustices and establishing resolutions.

Emotional Literacy

Emotional literacy is the ability to identify, understand, and respond to emotions in oneself and others in a healthy manner. The ability to name a feeling allows you to discuss and reflect with others about your personal experience of the world. The larger the emotional vocabulary, the more enhanced refinements you can make between feelings and the better you can communicate with others about your feelings. Adults who are able to label their emotions are on their way to becoming emotionally competent.

Once you are mindful of your painful feelings and you consciously take responsibility for them, see if your thoughts and actions trigger self-wounded feelings. Knowing this will enable you to make new choices that will be more loving to yourself.

Importance of Rapid Wound Care and Healing

The object of proper emotional wound care is to minimize the possibility of infection such as bitterness, resentment, revenge and hatred. Emotional infections cause the greatest obstructions to healing such as hopelessness, rage, depression, fear, addiction, violence and abuse.

Therefore, it is imperative that an emotional wound receives the same treatment as a physical injury, in order to heal most efficiently and minimize the appearance of scars. Furthermore, an efficient healing program will rapidly reduce personal, relational, employment and social problems.

Exercise: Unpleasant and Pleasant Feelings

Become familiar with the following Unpleasant or Negative Feelings and Pleasant or Positive Feelings. The purpose for developing your emotional literacy is to understand, identify and communicate your feelings. You must know how you feel in order to be able to meet your emotional needs. And you must communicate your feelings in order to get the emotional support and understanding you need from others, as well as to show your emotional support and understanding to them.

Emotional Literacy involves having self-awareness and recognition of one's own feelings and knowing how to manage them, such as the ability to stay calm when angered or to reassure oneself when in doubt.

Furthermore, emotions are your body's signal that needs are met or unmet. Pleasant emotions are felt when you believe that a need is being met and unpleasant emotions alert you to an unmet need.

Unpleasant or *Negative* Feelings

Anger	Depressed	Confused	Helpless
Irritated	Discouraged	Upset	Alone
Insulting	Ashamed	Doubtful	Paralyzed
Annoyed	Miserable	Uncertain	Useless
Upset	Disgusted	Perplexed	Empty
Bitter	Sulky	Skeptical	Vulnerable
Aggressive	Lousy	Unsure	Distressed
Resentful	Bad	Distrustful	Dominated
Provoked	Guilty	Uneasy	Inferior

Unpleasant or *Negative* Feelings

Indifference	Afraid	Hurt	Sad
Insensitive	Fearful	Rushed	Tearful
Neutral	Terrified	Tormented	Sorrowful
Reserved	Suspicious	Pained	Grief
Weary	Anxious	Injured	Anguish
Bored	Panic	Aching	Unhappy
Cold	Nervous	Victimized	Lonely
Disinterested	Scared	Alienated	Pessimistic
Preoccupied	Worried	Humiliated	Mournful

Pleasant or *Positive* Feelings

Open	Happy	Alive	Good
Confident	Joyous	Playful	Calm
Accepting	Thankful	Energetic	Peaceful
Free	Satisfied	Courageous	Comfortable
Sympathetic	Glad	Optimistic	Pleased
Interested	Important	Liberated	Relaxed
Satisfied	Delighted	Free	Blessed
Kind	Great	Wonderful	Encouraged
Reliable	Fortunate	Thrilled	Content

Pleasant or *Positive* Feelings

Love	Interested	Positive	Strong
Considerate	Concerned	Eager	Free
Affectionate	Affected	Keen	Sure
Sensitive	Intrigued	Determined	Certain
Tender	Inquisitive	Earnest	Unique
Devoted	Curious	Bold	Secure
Sympathy	Fascinated	Brave	Impulsive
Close	Engrossed	Optimistic	Tenacious
Passionate	Absorbed	Confident	Hardy

Take your time to learn and practice these skills: labelling your feelings, listening to feelings and asking feelings questions. With much practice, you will become fluent with the EQ language.

Case Studies of High-Impact Wounding

The following five stories illustrate the unmistakably, negative effect of high-impact wounding. These are not shameful or unusual stories. Living with open emotional wounds is no small problem! The stories are going to be continued later on, to show how those individuals overcame their emotional wounds.

Story #1: Sexual Abuse

At the age of six Brenda was sexually abused by a friend of the family. Obeying her mother's instructions to keep it a secret, Brenda buried the injury for half a century. At the age 56, she could no longer hide her emotional and physical pain. She had lived with depression, fear, shame, guilt, disgust, betrayal, loneliness, broken relationships and low self-esteem for years. The emotional pain became so severe that she could no longer bear the hurt on her own. For many years, she suffered with physical pain in her knees, shoulders and gums that could not be medically explained.

Story #2: Suicide Witness

The suicide episode Jessie witnessed at the mall left her emotionally traumatized for months. She had a strong support system, was proactive with the injury, talked to her family and friends, and used her journal to write down her thoughts and feelings about the episode. Her supports helped release a lot of the pain, but she was not able to let go of the "thump" sound caused by the impact of the man hitting the cement floor. For months, she suffered with post-traumatic symptoms, reliving the incident in her sleep. The "thump" sound continued to harass her mind for months. In desperate need for relief, she started psychotherapy and was introduced to the emotional cleansing tool.

Story #3: Workplace Harassment

Jack was 52 years of age and the principal of a large public school when he came to my office. Although he was generally liked, Jack had been severely harassed by three staff teachers over a two-year period. When he sought support from his superintendent, Jack was told to deal with the issues on his own. He tried, without success, to find a resolution with the teachers, but the harassment continued. Feeling emotionally exhausted and close to a nervous breakdown, Jack sought counselling. He felt hurt, anxious, depressed and in despair. He wanted to resign from his job and move on with his life.

Story #4: Severe Stomach Pain

An anxious mother called my office on behalf of her 15-year-old son, Mike. He had experienced intense stomach pains for nearly a week. Although medical examinations concluded that everything was fine, the throbbing did not stop. He became depressed and very anxious. For days, he had crying spells, and worried that he may fail in school and not do well as an adult. He stated; "I felt very sad and depressed. I had a very intense feeling of nervousness and didn't know what to do." He was fearful about up-coming life events, worried about his future plans and questioning if he would ever get married and have children. Absurd as it may sound - for this young teen, the worries were very real. (He scored 7 on the Scoring Key for the Emotional Pain Scale).

Story #5: Drug Addiction and Depression

Bill struggled with depression and addiction issues. He started drinking alcohol and smoking pot at the age of 13. At age 19, he turned to cocaine. Bill grew up in a good neighborhood, had friends, but never liked High

School. His parents were strict, demanding and emotionally detached. His mother was authoritative, critical and struggled with anger issues. Although Bill had a satisfying relationship with his father and two siblings, he often felt neglected by his father. Whenever his mother would wrongly accuse him of trouble making, his father would side with his mother. In his defense, Bill would react with rage and threaten to move. At the age of 20, his parents wanted him out of the house. He left the house in rage, and severed his relationship with his parents for three years. The feelings of anger, hurt and rejection continued to depress him. His drug habit escalated causing further problems in his life and relationships. Three years later and tired of suffering with depression and addiction issues, he came to my office for help.

These examples of intense emotional wounding demonstrate that open wounds can have a serious and negative impact on every aspect of a person's life. They also vividly underscore the fact that just ignoring the hurt will not cure the injuries. Without applying the correct treatment, there is little hope for healing and positive change. In my experience, no one desires to live with open sores. People yearn for their wounds to heal, but very few are aware of the proper step-by-step procedures that will make this possible.

Treatment Methods

Different types of emotional wounds may need different treatment, depending upon how they happened and how serious they are.

Low-Impact Wound: A low-impact wound such as an insult will require you to develop a strategic plan to address the injustice with the person. It is essential that such a plan be based on **changing yourself first**. When you choose to respond to a challenging situation rather than just reacting to it, your chances of being able to influence the situation positively are greatly increased.

You may get help to identify practical strategies that shift your behaviors and responses by consulting with a trusted friend or a counselor.

Talking about or debriefing the hurtful experience provides a channel to release the mixture of unpleasant emotions, thus relieving the negative pressure of the wound. Once this pressure is released, you are able to formulate a plan to address the inappropriate behavior. Never give up, even if the situation does not immediately improve. We learn by a process of trial and error. If you do not achieve the desired results with your first strategy, go "back to the drawing board" to explore other ways in which you could change yourself or influence the person who insulted you. For instance, if your partner keeps belittling you, setting a personal boundary by saying that you do not appreciate such remarks and do not want to hear them anymore is appropriate. If the behavior persists once you have established a clear boundary, involving a third party would be the next step. A trusted friend, manager or counselor could act as a mediator.

Journaling your hurtful feelings is another effective approach to relieving pressure from the wound. I encourage my clients to use both talking and journaling as "de-pressurizing" tools.

As a note of caution, do not try to hold the pressure in. Time alone will not cure the wound. It takes a lot of energy to hold on to hurt. In the long run, holding the hurt or grudge against someone else can hurt you just as much, and sometimes more than it hurts them.

Applying the **forgiveness** medicine to your open wound is also an important step. It is the most rapid and effective healing product. Forgiveness does not mean accepting an injustice or excusing poor behavior – it is a medicine that helps heal your wound.

High-Impact Wound: A high-impact wound such as long-term workplace harassment, domestic assault, abuse of any type, marital affair, tragic loss or harsh injustice will require a specialized wound care program. Using the traditional "talk, journal and forgive" tools on High-Impact Wounds may be insufficient in accomplishing complete healing.

In my clinical experience, I have found little success with the talk-journal-forgive approach. Instead, this approach involves long-term therapy and is often very slow and painstaking - for both client and therapist. Because healing results are slow to attain, clients often lose motivation and terminate therapy prematurely. Also, it is an expensive vehicle that most people cannot afford.

STEP 1

Cleansing the Wounds

"Writing is Cleansing – Cleansing is Healing"

Now it's time to learn how to clean your emotional wound. Let me give you a word picture to help explain the process.

Have you ever hand-washed a stubborn grass stain from your favorite pair of jeans? How did you remove the stain? What was your trick?

You probably washed the stain with water, soap and a brush. As you brushed the stain, the dirt slowly released itself from the jeans and disappeared down the drain. A stubborn stain may have required soaking for a period of time before washing. Most importantly, you were determined to scrub the grass stain until it was completely gone.

Likewise, you will clean your emotional injury by "washing out" or "writing out" the toxins from your wound. As you write your story, the emotional toxins are released and transferred to the written page. Thus, the healing process begins.

A Note of Caution:

You may experience increased moodiness and irritability during this time. If this is the case, go easy on yourself and with the people in your life. Let them know that you may become irritable for periods of time and not to take your feelings/behaviors personally.

Some people may be experiencing such severe pain related to childhood abuse or a present devastating life event that they are not able to expose their feelings on their own. It is essential that you form a support system. It is not advisable to attempt to process the pain of severe abuse on your own. If you suspect that you may have deep, buried pain or if you are not able to feel your pain despite a genuine willingness to do so, it is important that you receive counselling while you work through the workbook. While this is a self-help process, this does not mean that you have to do it alone.

At this point I would like you to close your eyes and focus on your feelings. Are you feeling anger, tension, tightness, stress, anxiety, emptiness, loneliness, sadness, a headache or heartbreak? Breathe into the painful feelings and embrace them with deep compassion.

What is a Cleansing Letter?

- The CLEANSING LETTER is NOT a formal letter. It is not a friendship letter, business letter or a love letter. It is not a journal. Do not write an outline, worry about spelling mistakes, grammar or any other rules you have learned. Simply download (transcribe) "word for word" what you have always wanted to say to the person who injured you. If the pain was caused by a catastrophic event, tragedy or illness, write down how this has made you feel.

- The cleansing letter is a tool that will guide the emotional cleansing process. It is a conversation between you and the person(s) or event(s) that injured you. Finally, you have a chance to tell your entire story.

- YES! Everything you have held back and tried to forget. Everything you have always wanted to share, but were afraid to disclose. Everything, yes, even the most hurtful and shameful thoughts you have carried for so long. Nobody will criticize you, reject you, blame you or think that you are making up a story.

- You may be thinking: "Wow, that's great! Finally, I get my chance to tell the truth, to say it all. But what about all the angry thoughts that I still have toward this person? I'll feel guilty for saying what I truly feel about him/her". Whatever you are thinking and feeling toward this person is normal. No matter how negative your thoughts are, nobody, not even God, will discredit you or think any less of you.

- It is very important that you disclose every thought and feeling. Do not hold anything back. Make sure that you clean every part of the wound. The entire bruise must be cleansed. Do not leave any part of the bruise unwashed. Unclean spots will re-infect the rest of the wound and prevent further healing.

Various theorists believe that putting pent-up worries, traumas or feelings on paper releases and discharges them, providing great relief. Some think that in writing about such concerns people gain distance, objectivity, perspective, and sometimes solutions. Personally, I think there is another reason: Writing about your feelings acknowledges and honors your feelings. These are typically disowned in shame-based people (i.e., people who feel bad to the core). Writing about your feelings is a way of loving yourself and love heals emotional wounds.

Using the Cleansing Tool

A Place to Write

Find a place that is comfortable, private and non-intrusive. You may decide on your favorite room in the house, a quite spot at the library or a secluded place in your much-loved natural environment.

Exercise: List the People and Events

List the people and events that have caused you emotional pain, pain which you still feel today.... emotional pain that has not gone away, that you have been holding for too long. Do not forget to include your name. You will write the final letter to your adult self. I will explain this at a later point. For now, complete the list, including your name.

Name Every **Person** Who Has Caused You Pain	Name Every **Event** that Has Caused You Pain

Begin Writing the Cleansing Letter

Exercise: Writing Cleansing Letters

- From your list of people and events, decide which person or event that you want to address first, including yourself. Write a separate letter to each person or event.

- Begin the letter by addressing the person, such as: "Dear Dad" or "Dear Mom." If you do not know or remember the person's name, "Hello" or "Dear Person" or just "Hi" would be appropriate.

- It is important that you stay focused. It's as if the person is with you in the room and you are telling him/her your story.

- Now that you have addressed the person and event, begin writing your story. Most people start their story at the place where the emotional injury took place. Others start writing from the present time, moving backward to the incident. Start wherever you feel most comfortable. Remember, the most important thing is to tell it all.

Additional Comments:

Several points to note while you disclose your painful events:

✓ Go through the stages of grief. Let the offence shock you, then let it completely hurt you. Do not avoid the pain. Sit with it and feel it no matter how unbearable it is. Please know it will end in time. Just feel it like a toothache and soon enough it will transition into something bearable.

✓ Let the offence make you angry. Do not lash out or you will feel guilty. Talk about it in the letter. Say that you are angry and your emotions are not under control. Do not feel bad for being angry. The last thing you need is shame and guilt. If you need to get physical, punch a pillow to make it through. Then anger, like the pain, will lessen over time.

✓ After being angry, accept what has been done. Accept it as fact and do not over analyze it. It happened. This will be shocking at first, but in time, you will accept it as a fact that you cannot change.

Personal Emotional Healing Experience

The following letter is written by a single mother, age 50, who suffered from post-traumatic symptoms related to a break-and-enter robbery. One night, her daughter's ex-boyfriend broke into her house and awakened her. Horrified by the intrusion, she suffered with severe depression, anxiety and post-traumatic disorder for nearly 14 months.

"When it was suggested to me that I write a 'cleansing' letter and forgive the person who had terrified me and brought me to the brink of self-destruction, I was absolutely flabbergasted, angry, confused and offended. Why did I have to forgive this person? Why was it up to me to make the effort - the first kind gesture in the whole situation? It just didn't seem right at all. It seemed that I would be caving in....falling prey again to being vulnerable and opening up to a place where I may be attacked again. I'm not sure how I would be attacked, but I had put up defenses and writing such a letter seemed to me that I would be cutting off my only way to survive.

Hell, I had just gotten to a place where I was not barricading the doors and windows or walking around with a knife. How could I forget all that had happened in order to "cleanse" myself? It did not make any sense at all to me.

But, because of a wonderful person showing me how to cope with a traumatic, life changing challenge, I was willing to try. Only because it seemed I could not move any further ahead. I was at a crossroad, but I didn't even know it. The suggestion seemed too bizarre to work, but I trusted enough to figure I had nothing to lose at that point.

I was told to choose someone I trusted to be there in the room or the next room just in case it was too overwhelming for me to relive. I chose a friend whom I knew would let me work this out, let me cry or scream, even be afraid again, and would just help me feel safe enough to go back to that morning.

I was told to write and just keep writing. Spelling, grammar, nothing else was important... just write out what had happened, how I felt, what that person had done, every little detail as well as how it had impacted me and my family, at the time, immediately afterwards and up to the point of writing the letter.

The first sentence was the hardest. After that, I ended up writing 8 pages. Eight pages of how I truly felt towards this person. I wrote, telling him of everything that had now changed because of his actions. But mainly, I wrote how I would not let him continue hovering in my life, always in the background, causing me fear, anxiety and anger.

Writing this letter gave me the courage to become a better person, a braver person, to know I could forgive him in order to cleanse the dirt he had brought into my life. I had no choice as to what he had done, but now I had a choice as to how I would remove the aftermath of the chaos that had been created. Having a choice gave me a power over my own life, over my own feelings and truly released me from the bondage that was surrounding me.

I took the letter to the scene of the crime and burned it. Right there and then, I swept the ashes out the door. With the ashes, I swept away the final bitterness that was in my heart and that was replaced with a calm that had been lacking for quite some time. This does not mean that I'm cured. At times, I still experience some of those feelings. But now, I can take them out, examine them, and put them back with the knowledge I have learned. Writing the cleansing letter gave me the safest way to feel freedom. It was not easy, but I would do it again in an instant for any other circumstances that require forgiveness of someone who harmed me in any way.

Where would I be today if I had not written that letter? Well, I would not be able to face life on life's terms. I would still have fear and anger in my heart. I think the worst part would be that I would still be a victim. Now, instead, I am an advocate of living life, instead of cowering behind vicious people and their own demons. I would not be able to be an example to my children of how to overcome hate, much of which was my own.

I would not have been able to show people that it's okay to reach out when I felt so alone. To not only rely on friends and family, but sometimes to realize that professionals can become the rock to lean upon and learn from, so that I may be able to pass along the wisdom I receive.

To write such a letter, at least for me, took more courage than anything I have ever done before, because I had to face my own fears. First, to identify them, truly face them, and to give them a name, so that I could learn to deal with them. I have learned more about myself... that is where I really am from writing this letter."

Getting Unstuck and Moving On

Are you having trouble getting started? If you started writing and the words are coming to you, skip this section and go to 'Checking In'. The following step is only for the person who is feeling stuck and is struggling to get started on the letters.

Most people find this part of the assignment most difficult. It is as if your brain and emotions are paralyzed or frozen - unable to think and feel. Finally, you get your chance to tell your side of the story and you cannot talk or feel. This part can be very frustrating. But, I don't want you to worry. What you are experiencing is uncomfortable, yet very normal.

Before you continue, stop and give yourself a minute to de-stress. I want you to relax, slow down your thoughts, calm your emotions and take a deep breath. Yes, right now! Take a deep breath and slowly INHALE and EXHALE. Repeat this step until you feel more relaxed.

Are you relaxed? Great! If not, do more breathing exercises. If you still find yourself overly anxious, frustrated or numb, give yourself a break and come back at a later time.

Now that you are relaxed, you may be thinking: "I don't know where to start?" or "What do I say, I haven't seen or talked to the person in years."

No problem! Keep reading.

I want you to focus and listen to what you are thinking and feeling right at this moment as you are staring at the person's name or the event. Listen to the voice or conversation you are having in your mind. Focus inside your body; attend to the physical sensations. Breathe into any painful feelings, embracing them with deep compassion. Is there tension, tightness, fluttering, emptiness, aloneness, loneliness, sadness, heartache, and heartbreak?

What comes to your mind when you think about the person or event? What are you hearing yourself say right now? What are you feeling?

You may be thinking: "I don't want to talk to you! You hurt me!! I hate what you did to my life!" Or, "I still don't know what to tell you. Actually, what I want to say, I'm too ashamed to write." Or, "I love you, and feel too guilty to share my negative thoughts with you. I don't want to hurt your feelings."

Are you hearing your thoughts? If yes - Great! Your mind is alive and active. You are having a conversation. Start writing your thoughts and feelings, right now – word for word. Keep going. What is your next thought and feeling? Whatever it is, write it down. What do you want to say to the person? What do you want him or her to know about you?

Keep going. By now, you may be blurting it all out. It may sound like emotional diarrhea. Don't worry, you are doing great. Just keep going. Don't stop until everything is out.

I caution you not to overwhelm yourself. This is very hard work and may take some time. As with any large project, make sure to take lots of breaks. There is no need to rush this one.

Again, remember, it is very important that you disclose every thought and feeling. Do not hold anything back.

If you are stuck in the anger, blame, depression or numbness of your wounded self, you need to find a bridge. Bridges are things you can do to open your emotions. Of the many bridges you can use, prayer, especially a prayer of gratitude, is probably the most powerful bridge. Prayer can take many forms, such as dialogue, meditation, recitation or song. The choice is up to you. Some people have found that repeating a simple prayer of gratitude throughout the day helps them stay open emotionally.

If you are too stuck in your wounds to pray from your heart, or you don't believe in prayer, then you need to try other bridges that can open your emotions. These include:

- Listening to music
- Taking a walk
- Watch a movie on emotional traumas and abuse.
- Talking with a friend
- Reading spiritual literature
- Journaling
- Drawing or doing other artwork like sculpture or collage
- Dancing
- Attending Twelve Step or other support group meetings
- Playing with a child or a pet
- Being held by a loving person
- Letting yourself cry
- Releasing your anger alone by yelling and pounding into a pillow

Checking In

Now that you are writing, make sure that you gradually go back to the time and place where the injury or hurt occurred.

Unlocking the doors and washing the filth from your life is tough work. Keep going. It is only a matter of time until all of your emotions are clean. And once cleansed, you will furnish your emotional life with refreshing and revitalizing activities that will brighten your life.

As you continue with your story, release all the toxins, including feelings of pain, hurt, shame, guilt, anger, fear, anxiety, worry, depression and lost memories.

For Brenda, Jessie, Jack, Mike and Bill, the process of writing unlocked the doors to their hidden life that were packed with anguish, hurt, fear, depression, anxiety and obscurity. Through writing, the emotional toxins and negative energy were released from their wounds.

Story #1: Sexual Abuse

Brenda wrote two letters, one to a male family friend and one to her mother. She told the family friend how his inappropriate sexual acts nearly destroyed her emotional life. Life was precious to her and she was not going to give in to suicide. She expressed how she had lived in constant fear and that it was difficult to trust people. She was a fighter, a cold and defensive person. There was no room in her heart to love another person. This room was restricted and forbidden to the outside world. She talked about her sufferings - how her emotional pain travelled throughout her body trying to find a way of escape. Unable to find release, the pressure of the pain intensified, causing Brenda to live with chronic symptoms for nearly 45 years. After she completed the letters, her most painful weight was finally released.

Story #2: Suicide Witness

In her conversation, Jessie went back to the mall and "confronted" the man who committed suicide. She wrote to him telling him how she felt about what he had done. She hated him for traumatizing her. She let him know that he was selfish in not thinking about his consequences. How his actions hurt her, haunted her and made her life extremely difficult. That she had to take time off from work because she was not able to cope and accomplish the simple things of life. Jessie found some release from writing the letter, but the final relief occurred when she discarded the letter at the mall.

Story #3: Workplace Harassment

Jack was skeptical about the whole cleansing program. He did not believe that the process of a written letter would help him with his emotional pain and problems at work. Despite his skepticism, he wrote three letters – one to his superintendent, and one to each teacher. In the letters, he spoke directly to each person and expressed every concern and issue that had troubled him for two years regarding his/her actions and bullying tactics. He talked about his disappointments and the emotional toll it took on his personal and professional life.

He also explained the elements needed not only to prevent workplace harassment, but also to promote the values and respectful conduct necessary in today's diverse workforce.

During the follow-up session, Jack explained that the writing process was both painful and empowering. It was painful in that he had to address the issues one more time, yet empowering, because it provided him the path to release the pain. There were no barriers to sabotage the conversations. He did not have to worry about saying it right, pleasing the bully or fearing further harassment. He was able to talk about his case, issues, hurts, and needs.

By speaking-out, he was able to release every hurt and emotional distress. Finally, the long-standing emotional filth or baggage was removed. The toxins were no longer a part of his life. The open wounds were now clean and ready to heal.

Story #4: Severe Stomach Pain

Mike could not wait to go home and write his letters. He had very personal and sensitive issues to discuss with people and himself. Some of the issues were too difficult and shameful to share with either his parents or his counselor. It was these issues that distressed him the most and sent frantic emotional shock waves through his body. Once released, his emotions stabilized.

Emotional shock waves or panic attacks are similar to earth tremors. Whenever our emotional body surpasses its maximum pressure threshold, the pressure valve releases, sending shock waves or panic attack symptoms throughout our body. Once Mike released the issues that caused such enormous stress to his body, his emotions stabilized. He stated, "After the letter, I felt that it helped me a lot. I felt less of the anxieties."

Story #5: Drug Addiction and Depression

Bill could not wait to release the anger, pain and guilt feelings he had carried for nearly 10 years. He addressed the first letter to his father. Because he shared a close relationship with him, he disclosed his guilt for walking out on him, how he missed spending time with him and that he felt sorry for him. He told him that he needed him to be assertive and a positive role model. He apologized for his harsh and negative attitude, for hurting him, for disrespecting him, and for troubling him with his addiction issues and poor manners.

He wrote the second letter to his mother. This letter was challenging and painful. He had a lot of hurt stored in his emotional bank account that needed release. He expressed his love for her and how hard it had been for him to share this with her. He had tried on numerous occasions, but her critical spirit would always sabotage his efforts.

He felt rejected, unworthy and a failure. She seemed so much stronger and impossible to please.

As the feelings of anger subsided, he was encouraged by his new feelings. He had not felt this relaxed and happy for a long time. Once he forgave his mother and apologized for his behaviors, he felt a need to visit her and make amends.

In a follow-up session, he happily disclosed how things had changed between his mother and him. I was pleased to hear that they are working on becoming good friends and that the painful struggles of the past are no longer a present issue.

Writing the Cleansing Letter to Your Inner-Child

What Exactly is this so-called Inner-Child?

The Inner-Child is not literally or physically real, but figuratively, metaphorically real. It represents your emotional reality – it is the "Feeler". The Adult-Self represents your cognitive reality – it is the "Thinker". In other words, your mind represents your Adult-Self and your emotions characterize the Inner-Child.

We were all children once, and still have that child dwelling within us. But most adults are quite unaware of this. The fact is that the majority of so-called adults are not truly adults at all. We all get older. Anyone, with a little luck, can do that. But, psychologically speaking, this is not adulthood. This lack of conscious awareness of our Inner-Child (our emotions) is precisely where so many behavioral, emotional and relationship difficulties stem from.

True adulthood hinges on acknowledging, accepting, and taking responsibility for loving and parenting our own Inner-Child. For most adults, this never happens. Instead, their inner-child has been ignored, belittled, abandoned or rejected.

We are told by society to "grow up," putting childish things aside. To become adults, we've been taught that our inner child—representing our child-like capacity for innocence, wonder, awe, joy, sensitivity and playfulness—must be stifled, confined or even killed.

The Inner-Child has positive qualities... peace, wholeness, joy, goodness, innate worth, feelings/emotions that are good and that make us human. But it also holds our accumulated childhood hurt, trauma, fears and anger. What we did not sufficiently receive from our parents, we must confront - painful though it may be. The past trauma, sadness, disappointments, anxieties, fears, losses and depression must be accepted. Becoming an adult means accepting that certain childhood needs were, spiteful or not, unmet by our imperfect parents or caretakers.

"Grown-ups" are convinced they have successfully outgrown and left this child - and its emotional baggage - long behind. But this is far from the truth. At the root are self-dislike, shame-based behaviors, fears, insecurities, loneliness, guilt, hurt, anger and low self-esteem.

In fact, most adults are constantly influenced or controlled by their Inner-Child or emotions. For many adults, it is not the Adult-Self (mind) guiding their lives, but rather an emotionally wounded Inner-Child (emotions). Some adults have a six-year-old running in a fifty-year-old frame. The Inner-Child is a hurt, angry, fearful little boy or girl calling the shots, and making adult decisions.

Still not convinced that you have an Inner-Child? Let me put it this way; how often do you criticize yourself for things that you do, or maybe don't do and feel that you should? A lot? How easy is it for you to look at yourself with pleasure in the mirror? Not easy? How much do you really like yourself - warts and all? Not much? If these were your answers then your Inner-Child is active. But feeling very sad, lost, lonely, and pretty small and insignificant.

The truth is the Inner-Child, though battered, covered, hurt and cut off, is alive. The child you once were, you still are (Leman and Carson 1989).

Uniting Your Inner Child

Getting in touch with our Inner-Child is not always easy. At first it might seem that he or she just wants to cry and cry. This is natural. The parts of us that were split off at a young age had to go away for good reasons— abuse, fear, neglect, and misunderstanding. These young parts were not allowed to express their overwhelming feelings, so they took the feelings away with them.

The goal is to reunite your Inner-Child with your Adult-Self. When love is in short supply, can the fragmented relationship between the Adult-Self and Inner-Child heal? The answer is yes. The cure, quite simply, is love. Love heals and provides the foundation of growth and life. Although the Adult-Self operates logically, the Inner-Child hungers for love, and continues to cry out until that hunger is satisfied.

One approach uses writing to start the reunion of your present Adult-Self and your Inner-Child. I call this "conversational journaling." The purpose of this exercise is to find and connect with your Inner-Child to bring about healing, happiness and the feeling of being loved.

It is through healing your Inner-Child, and by grieving the wounds that you suffered, that you can change your behavior patterns and clear your emotional process. You can release the grief with its pent-up rage, shame, terror and pain from those feeling places which exist within you.

You need to rescue, nurture and love your Inner-Child. It is necessary to own and honor the child who you were in order to love the person you are today. You do this by owning and honoring your Inner-Child's experiences and feelings and releasing the emotional energy that you are still carrying around.

Exercise: Naming your Inner-Child

To make this relationship concept more realistic, you will need to give your Inner-Child a name.

Name of Your Inner-Child: _____.

Quotes: The following are inspirational quotes related to releasing your Inner-Child:

Happy is he who still loves something he loved in the nursery: He has not been broken in tow by time; he is not two men, but one, and he has saved not only his soul but his life. ~G.K. Chesterton

So, like a forgotten fire, a childhood can always flare up again within us. ~Gaston Bachelard

When I grow up I want to be a little boy. ~Joseph Heller, Something Happened, 1974

Inner-Child–Adult-Self Illustration

In the following illustration, I named the Inner-Child: ***Johnny*** and the Adult-Self: ***John***. *Johnny* (inner child) and *John* (adult self) have their first written conversation.

John (Adult-Self)

Shares his **THOUGHTS**
(What he is **thinking**)

Johnny (Inner-Child)

Shares his **EMOTIONS**
(What he is **feeling**)

The conversation will mainly focus on *Johnny's* feelings and *John's* false beliefs. *Johnny* shared about what it had been like living with *John*. He told him about the lack of love he felt from John, his parents and care givers. Also, he shared his disappointments, failures, hurtful experiences, successes and happy memories. *John* shared his false beliefs he learned when he was very young. He defined himself and the conclusions he drew about himself, others, the world, etc., as a result of his difficult childhood experiences. *John* falsely concluded that he was bad, unlovable and unworthy. He rejected *Johnny* and in return felt rejected by others.

John used the following questions to help Johnny share his feelings; his stories:

- Do you feel unconditionally loved by me? Why not?
- Do you feel completely accept by me? Why not?
- Do I help you meet all your needs, wants and desires? Why not?
- Are you truly happy with me? Why not?
- Do I truly believe, value, and respect you? Why not?
- Do you feel safe and protected? Why not?

Sample Letter to John

Hi John,

I feel strange writing to you. I have lived with you for so long and we have never had a one-on-one, heart-to-heart conversation. I have tried hundreds of times to talk to you, I begged you to listen to me, but you ignored me, told me to wait, criticized me or told me to shut up. Don't get me wrong, I'm not complaining. I just need to tell you what has been going on in my life with you. I like you, I mean I want to love you so much, but it has been hard. So, please listen to what I have to tell you. All I need from you is to listen. You can ask questions, if you don't understand something or to help me when I'm stuck. OK?

As I have said, I like you a lot, but I have been hurting, sad, lonely, put down . . .

Exercise: Writing the Cleansing Letter to Yourself

Start writing your own letter. Now that you have named your Inner-Child, let your Inner-Child talk to your Adult-Self (you). As you invite your lost Inner-Child back into your life, be ready for him or her to express a lot of distress.

You need to take his or her feelings extremely seriously. "Soothing" the child does not mean saying, "*There, there, dear. It's OK. Stop crying.*" You may have heard voices like that in your past, but your job is to be a different kind of parent, one who really listens to the child's feelings. The first part of soothing is to hear the feelings. The child might not be able to tell you why she or he feels sad or angry or scared.

Your job is to listen to your Inner-Child's story, pay attention to the feelings and be very supportive. Your Inner-Child may need your help throughout the conversation. Always wait for him or her to ask you for help, before you offer your guidance. It is important that you create a safe environment for your Inner-Child, by giving him or her permission to be truly honest and transparent with you.

If you can, find a safe and quiet place where you can sit down, listen and write out your conversation. Let the feelings emerge. Accept all of them, even though it is painful. If you cannot bear all of the feelings at once, tell your Inner-Child that you will listen for ten minutes, or five, or two minutes. Then promise the child that you will continue at a later time.

As the feelings emerge, focus on loving your Inner-Child who is entrusting you with these valuable and vulnerable emotions. Tell your Inner-Child that you are proud of her or him for coming forth. At times, you may feel completely overwhelmed. You may feel like "you are a child" or you are acting "like a child". If you feel this way, that's very normal. Try to stay in this place. Don't try to hide or run away. See if you can create an inner shift where you can feel a little more like a grownup holding your Inner-Child.

Some people may not be aware that they carry deep and hidden emotional pain linked to childhood. Others may feel too overwhelmed and fear losing control when they connect with their emotional agonies. It is not advisable to attempt to open up to the pain of severe abuse on your own. You want to establish a safe support system, preferably with a person of the same sex, who is sensitive and emotionally mature.

If you suspect that you may have deep buried pain or if you have not succeeded in feeling your pain despite a genuine willingness to do so, it is imperative that you receive therapeutic help while you work through the workbook. While this is a self-help process, this does not mean that you have to do it alone. Part of being a loving adult is asking for help when help is needed.

Know when Your Emotional Wound is Clean

You may be wondering and asking yourself the following questions: "How will I know when my emotional toxins are gone? When are my cleansing letters completed?"

Because you are dealing with an invisible wound, you will not be able to see the final results, as you would with a physical wound. You may be asking: "Then how will I know?"

When you have said everything you wanted and needed to say to the person(s) or events (s). When it is all said and done. When you come to a point where there is nothing else to say. You will know your wound is clean when you have run out of words. Once you have disclosed everything and your pen stops writing.

At this point you may have doubts and question the validity of this exercise. You may be wondering if your emotional wounds are thoroughly cleansed or if you missed a spot.

The following two-step process will help you test the cleanliness of your emotional wounds:

1) Read your letters – preferably out load and feel the wound(s) one more time.

2) While you read your letters, stay mindful of your feelings. If you feel overwhelmed, angry, hurt, sad or any other unpleasant feelings with any part of the letters, continue writing (talking) about what you are feeling.

If no other unpleasant feelings were provoked and you have nothing more to say after reading your letters, your wounds are fully cleansed.

Congratulations!!

You just completed the hardest step of the emotional wound-care process. Great Job! I want you to be very proud of yourself. The emotional toxins will no longer hurt you.

However, you will continue to feel pain because your emotional wounds are still exposed. The emotional pain will slowly fade away as your emotional wounds heal.

Take a moment to pause and reflect on your great achievement. Your emotional wounds are CLEAN. You removed all the toxins and poisons from within you.

Before you start rebuilding the parts of your life that have been wounded, you will have to destroy the cleansing letters.

STEP 2

Destroying the Toxins

Yes, you get to destroy your cleansing letters!

For most people, step two is the most exhilarating part of the emotional wound-care process. Here, you will get to put an end to all the misery and emotional viruses that have held you prisoner for too long. You will get to destroy them once and for all.

Since emotional viruses are active and alive, I find that the best method to destroy the toxins is by burning them. Fire is still one of the best disinfectors and cleansers. If this method is too frightening or strange for you, not to worry, there are other ways to get rid of the emotional viruses.

Let's see how our stories were concluded...

Story #1: Sexual Abuse

Brenda decided to go back to the house where she was raised. While standing at the sidewalk and facing the front of the house, she noticed a girl standing behind the bedroom window, waiving at her. The girl was smiling and looked cheerful. Brenda quickly recognized that the girl at the window was her little inner child. Observing her smile, she knew that everything was going to be ok from now on. Yet, at the same moment, she was shocked when she realized that all this time, her little girl lived in the house where the sexual abuse originally took place.

Nearly 45 years being away from each other, Brenda found her lost little girl smiling with joy. That evening, the two re-connected with an enormous embrace and burned the letters on the front lawn of the house. Because it was winter, she was able to burn the letters in a safe place in the snow. It was here she experienced her biggest release, where she put an end to the old life and a beginning to the new.

In her final counselling session, Brenda explained that her long-standing depression and anxiety symptoms vanished. She was excited about her future. She talked about building trust and honesty in her intimate relationships, starting with her inner child, her partner, her family members, her friends and her Heavenly Father.

Story #2: Suicide Witness

Jessie faced her trauma head on by going back to the place where the suicide occurred - letter in hand. She threw the letter into a garbage can that just happened to be located at the exact place where the man fell. Here, she released every negative emotion associated to the trauma and reclaimed her harmony with the specific spot in the mall.

Story #3: Workplace Harassment

Still somewhat skeptical, Jack burned the letters in the fireplace of his house. He explained how difficult it was to get the paper to burn. It was as difficult as lighting damp paper. Once the paper burned to ashes, he experienced another big emotional release. Standing by the fireplace, he realized that the toxins were not only released from his body, but were also destroyed in the fire. This is when Jack knew that he was going to be fine; that he had released it all and that it was gone. The toxins were no longer going to hurt him.

Story #4: Severe Stomach Pain

Mike shredded the letters during one of his counselling sessions. Mike saw the act of shredding as a way of destroying the toxins and the poisonous plant in his life. Also, he needed support with the prayer of forgiveness. He did not want to do this step on his own and behind closed doors. Because the emotional trauma occurred in undisclosed locations, he felt that he needed to destroy the terrible incidents in the presence of his therapist. Step two helped Mike sanitize a wounded chapter in his life.

It washed his wounds and destroyed the venom that caused terrifying pain in his stomach and anxiety for nearly two weeks. (He scored 2 on the Scoring Key for the Emotional Pain Scale).

Story #5: Drug Addiction and Depression

Bill found such emotional release through writing, he was thrilled to burn the letters and put an end to the painful past. He felt clean, refreshed and ready to restore his life. Stopping the drug habit and rebuilding his severed relationships was no longer an impossible goal to achieve.

At the end of treatment, Bill had been drug free for two months, was rebuilding his relationships and feeling happy. All symptoms of depression had diminished.

Burning, Shredding or Discarding

Give yourself time to think about the different options that are available to you in destroying your letters. Most people prefer to burn the letters. Your letters represent an unkind, difficult and, for some of you, brutal chapter in your life.

Ask yourself: "How would I want to destroy the letters?" Whatever method you decide to use, allow this step to be special and meaningful.

Do not rush this part of the process. You are getting ready to flush away and destroy the hurt and injustice.

Decision Making Techniques:

- Listen to your Inner-Child and Spirit and let them decide for you.

- Follow your gut feelings. What is your gut telling you?

- Talk it over with your counselor or best friend.

- Write out your options and evaluate by listing pros/cons.

- Pray and seek guidance from your Heavenly Father.

Exercise: Choose Your Discard Option – see next page.

Write down your discarding option: #_____.

Go ahead and burn, shred or discard your letter(s). Take your time.

a) Burning the Cleansing Letters

1) Locate a safe place to burn your cleansing letters such as: a fireplace, your backyard, a cottage, near a lake or in a fire pit.
2) Light the paper.
3) Watch the flames burn the cleansing letters.
4) Watch the flames destroy the toxins.
5) Watch the cleansing letters and toxins turn to ashes.
6) Discard the ashes.

b) Shredding the Cleansing Letters

1) Locate a paper shredder.
2) Shred the cleansing letters.
3) Watch the toxins get shredded.
4) Discard the shredding.

c) Discarding the Cleansing Letters

1) Rip-up the letters.
2) Discard the letters into the garbage or
3) Flush the letters down the toilet.

Congratulations! You *cleansed* your emotional wounds and ***destroyed*** the toxins. How are you feeling? At this stage of the healing journey, people start to feel relief, like a heavy weight has been lifted off their shoulders.

STEP 3

Treating the Wounds

Now that you have destroyed the cleansing letters, you are ready to apply the disinfectant ointment, which I call forgiveness. This must be done immediately after you have destroyed the cleansing letter, as the emotions will quickly form a seal over the wound.

Open wounds stay contaminated to some extent and are potential sites for further emotional infection. The best way to prevent infection is to disinfect the wounds and discourage further growth of emotional bacteria such as bitterness, resentment, revenge and anger.

Forgiveness and Letting Go

Forgiveness is the **final disinfectant** or **antiseptic ointment** that can completely wash/heal emotional wrongdoings and open wounds. You will learn how to apply the medicine to your emotional wound. This ointment is for your own use and when permitted, can be applied to other people.

At this stage, you might be thinking: "Did he say – I need to forgive? If I forgive it feels like I am also saying they had the right to do me wrong. It does not feel right that I have to forgive somebody who really has no idea that they did wrong."

You are right. You are doing the hard work of forgiving them and they have no idea they wronged you, or worse, they don't honestly care. So why forgive?

Well, there are many reasons, but I am going to focus on four:

- First, forgiveness is a pleasurable experience. It feels much better than anger or hate. Forgiveness is a powerful gift for those who have been hurt. The experience of truly forgiving somebody can make you happier than living with anger for the rest of your life.

- Second, forgiveness removes you from being entangled in the injustice or malice that hurt you in the first place. If it was a bad business deal, you break free of it and maintain your integrity. If it was a family member talking behind your back, you release the hurt, set new boundaries and maintain your wellbeing. Forgiveness sets you free from being bogged down in knee-deep mud.

- Third, you open yourself up to amazing possibilities for a happy life. When you do not forgive, you draw the curtains in your soul and your life gets dark. When you forgive, you let the light in again, and you go on with your life in peace.

- Lastly, the greatest thing about forgiveness is, it allows you to love again. It will allow you to love and be loved. Forgiveness is tough, for sure, but love is infinitely more valuable than the pain forgiveness costs. No matter what you have to go through to forgive, you are getting a steal of a deal to be able to love and be loved again.

"All this sounds good," you may be telling yourself, *"How can I ever forget what the person did to me? You do not forget!"* I agree with you, you will never forget. You will probably always remember the particular injustice done to you. However, forgiveness is not the same as forgetting. When you apply the forgiveness medicine to your emotional wound, the intense emotions associated with the event begin to fade and heal.

Jean Monbourquette (2000) suggests considering the 12 steps to forgiveness as a way to heal our pain. He encourages forgiving ourselves first, then sometimes forgiving the other person by renewing the relationship when possible and desired.

12 Steps to Forgiveness

Step 1: Do not take revenge and put an end to all hurtful acts. Avoid resentment and revenge – these only lead to dead ends. Do everything you can to stop any unfair or hurtful act.

Step 2: Acknowledge what has hurt you. Delve deeply within and find the courage to get in touch with the resulting pain.

Step 3: Share your pain with someone. Be careful not to retreat into isolation. Share the burden of your pain with someone in order to see more clearly within.

Step 4: Clearly identify your loss in order to grieve it. Take an inventory of the losses that result from what has hurt you. Realize that sometimes we are more hurt by our own interpretation of an event than by the event itself.

Step 5: Accept your anger. Try to see your anger as a positive force that sounds the alarm, warns you of danger, and leads you to discover the values held closest to your heart.

Step 6: Forgive yourself. Forgive your Adult-Self and your Inner-Child. Accept yourself with your limitations and weaknesses. Restore peace within yourself – between your Adult-Self and your Inner-Child first, in order to be able to forgive others.

Step 7: Understand the other person. Try to look at the other person with fresh eyes. See that the other person has his/her own pain. Hurt people have a tendency to hurt other people.

Step 8: Find meaning in what has hurt you. Think about a positive meaning to attach to the pain; discover a new part of yourself.

Step 9: Know that you are worthy of forgiveness. Recall the care that others have shown you through their forgiveness. Draw on this unique sentiment in order to feel worthy of forgiveness.

Step 10: Stop withholding forgiveness. Just do it and keep it simple.

Step 11: Be open to the grace of forgiveness. This step is subject to each person's own spirituality, even though the author approaches it from a religious point of view. Avoid seeking glorification in forgiveness or giving up all power. Find your source of inspiration to forgive; your core values, your life's mission or a creative drive.

Step 12: Decide either to end the relationship or to renew it. Consider your future relationship with the other person. Either let it go, wishing him/her great happiness, or establish a new alliance.

In conclusion, forgiveness does not mean returning to how things were before you were hurt. Forgiveness allows you to heal and create something different.

Forgiveness is not a feeling. It is a decision. It is a decision you make when you are ready to apply forgiveness - the disinfectant ointment to the open wound. Once you decide to apply the ointment, the medicine will carry out what it is designed to do. Even if it is not easy to apply and you feel more short term throbbing, you have the determination of knowing that the alternative is even harder.

No matter how justified you feel about your point of view regarding the situation, an unhealed emotional wound will continue to hurt you and further negatively impact your life.

- You will not go another day baring the pain.
- You will no longer ignore the infection: the grudge, the bitterness, the resentment, the revenge and the anger.
- You will apply the medicine of forgiveness.
- You will protect the clean emotional wounds.
- You will not re-injure your emotional wounds.
- You will not allow others to re-injure your wounds.

Making a Promise to Yourself

Promise yourself that no matter what the reason:

As the ointment begins to work itself through the wound, you will start to feel better. Initially, forgiveness is not a feeling, but a decision.

Promise yourself that no matter the reason, you'll try to stay on the road of forgiveness. The benefits of applying the forgiveness medicine to your wounds go far beyond anything you can imagine at this moment. Your emotional wounds will heal and you will have the liberty to continue to develop into the person of your dreams. Make peace and let your emotions heal. Let your Inner-Child heal.

Once applied, your wounds will start to heal and your emotional pain will start to ease.

You will feel:

- A new sense of relief.
- A greater degree of emotional release.
- A better sense of inner peace.
- More relaxed, calmer and loving.
- An improved level of mood and energy.
- A weight off your shoulder – lightened.
- A disconnection and detachment to the injustice.
- A greater sense of freedom.
- An improved self-esteem and confidence.

A Spiritual Approach to Forgiveness

Spiritual foundations and skills can help reduce symptoms. For example, one who understands infinite, divine love might find it easier to love and forgive others and self. Respect and regard for all humans might help one understand unconditional human worth. Peace of conscience, forgiveness, and a spiritual perspective can help heal the emotional wounds.

Forgiveness gives you a taste of what it feels like to be God, and it is a terrific feeling. God forgave us because it gave Him pleasure to do so. He was happy to do so. Love forgives, and so does God, and so can you.

From here, you are at a place to forgive. It will be hard work, but it is worth it. Sit and pray for the person you have hated. Sit and imagine them with a good life, them coming to realize that what they did was wrong, maybe not to you, but to somebody, perhaps to God. Then be willing to love them in your heart. Want the best for them. Hope for the best for them. Stop praying for God to destroy them and pray for God to bless them. Pray for God to open up their hearts so they can receive the love that will stop them from hurting others.

Exercise: Apply the Forgiveness Medicine

When you are ready, apply the forgiveness medicine directly to the emotional wounds by following the prayer on the next page. If you feel uncomfortable using the prayer, feel free to create your own version or words of forgiveness.

Verbalizing your prayer is a crucial component of the healing process. Forgiveness is the medicine and prayer applies it.

Prayer of Self-Forgiveness

"God, forgive _____ (Me and Johnny) _____
                              [Name your adult-self and inner-child]

for _____ (hurting, neglecting, hating, abusing, criticizing, shaming, etc.) _____
                     [Name the injustice, the abuse, the injury]

and for what _____ (I and Johnny) _____ are/were
not aware of doing.   [Name your adult-self and inner-child]

Forgive me for hurting myself by holding on to the infections and not looking after my emotions, (Inner-Child) and my thoughts (Adult-Self). Thank You for the Gift of Forgiveness - for cleansing and healing my emotions (Inner-Child) and my thoughts (Adult-Self). Amen."

Prayer of Other-Forgiveness

"God, forgive _____
                              [Name the person]

For _____ and
                     [Name the injustice, the abuse, the injury]

for what _____is/was not aware of doing.
                     [Name the person]

Forgive me for hurting myself in holding on to the infections and not looking after after my emotions. Thank You for the Gift of Forgiveness – for cleansing and healing my emotions. Amen."

Congratulations!!

You have completed the cleansing steps. I want you to be very proud of yourself for completing these brave and difficult steps. Now you are forgiven and have forgiven the person who injured you. Your emotional wounds are finally CLEAN – cleaner than fresh white snow. All the emotional toxins are gone and are no longer a part of your life.

Exercise: Name the Feelings

I feel _____
(relieved, calmer, more inner peace, relaxed, happier, clean, hopeful, excited, etc.).

At this same moment, you may also feel a certain amount of fear, vulnerability, uncertainty or insecurity.

Some of you may feel that your emotions are unprotected and exposed to further hurt and injury. The old protective devices are stripped and you have no other tools to protect your emotions. If this is you, your thoughts and feelings are normal.

The good news is that you do not need to worry. Step four will cover the essential tools to help you protect your emotional wounds and guard your emotional body from future hazards and threats of injustice.

Now that the wound is thoroughly cleaned with the antiseptic wash and treated with the antibiotic ointment, the final step will present six tools to help protect the wound until it is fully healed.

STEP 4

Protecting the Wounds

Now that your wounds are clean, we do not want to leave them open and unprotected. At this point of the process, your emotional wounds are fully exposed to all the healthy and harmful elements of life.

Goal: Become an expert in protecting your emotional wounds.

Setting Boundaries

Setting boundaries is essential if we want to be physically, emotionally and spiritually healthy. Creating healthy boundaries is empowering. By recognizing the need to set and enforce limits, you protect your wounds and self-esteem, maintain self-respect, and enjoy healthy relationships.

Unhealthy boundaries cause emotional pain that can lead to dependency, depression, anxiety, and even stress-induced physical illness. A lack of boundaries is like leaving the door to your home unlocked; anyone, including unwelcome guests, can enter at will.

On the other hand, having too rigid boundaries can lead to isolation, like living in a locked-up castle surrounded by a trench. No one can get in, and you cannot get out.

What are Boundaries?

The easiest way to think about a boundary is a property line. We have all seen "No Trespassing" signs, which send a clear message that if you violate that boundary, there will be consequences. This type of boundary is easy to picture and understand because you can see the sign and the border it protects. Personal boundaries can be harder to define because the lines are invisible, can change, and are unique to each individual.

Personal boundaries, just like the "No Trespassing" sign, define where you end and others begin. They are determined by the amount of physical and emotional space you allow between yourself and others. Personal boundaries help you decide what types of communication, behavior, and interaction are acceptable.

Variety of Personal Boundaries

Thought Boundaries: Thought boundaries provide a barrier between your thoughts and intruding thoughts. A thought boundary is used to protect and support your emotional wound. Its purpose is equal to a Band-Aid or a piece of material used to dress a physical wound or to wrap an injured limb. It provides a boundary and barrier to protect the wound from bacteria and re-injury.

Exercise: Setting Thought Boundaries

In your mind, set a "Thought Boundary" between the past injustice and your present life. Do the following:

1) Do not think or talk about the injury for the next four to six months. Set this rule with yourself and promise that; "I will freeze my thoughts by not thinking or talking about the injustice, not until the wound is fully healed".

2) This rule will establish a boundary to help rest the injury and the emotional wounds. Similar to a cast that protects a broken arm, the thought boundary will act as a barrier to guard, protect and rest your open wounds.

3) Set the same rule with your family members, circle of friends or anyone who is aware of your emotional wounds. Tell everyone that you will no longer think or talk about the injustice, not until you are fully healed.

4) Give your wounds a good rest. Put the injustice in a box and put it into storage or a freezer. Protect and nurse the wound and it will heal itself in the same way as a broken arm mends. Be patient and wait until it is fully healed, and then you can talk about it as much as you like.

Physical Boundaries: Physical boundaries include your body, sense of personal space, sexual orientation, and privacy. These boundaries are expressed through clothing, shelter, noise tolerance, verbal instruction, and body language.

An example of a physical boundary violation is a person who stands too close to you. Your immediate and automatic reaction is to step back in order to reset your personal space. By doing this, you send a non-verbal message that when this person stands too close, you feel an invasion of your personal space. If the person continues to move closer, you might verbally protect your boundary by telling him/her to stop crowding you.

Other examples of physical boundary invasions are:

- Inappropriate touching, such as unwanted sexual advances.

- Looking through others' personal files and emails.

- Not allowing others their personal space. (e.g., barging into your boss's office without knocking).

Emotional and Intellectual Boundaries: These boundaries protect your sense of self-esteem and ability to separate your feelings from others. When you have weak emotional boundaries, it's like getting caught in the midst of a hurricane with no protection. You expose yourself to being greatly affected by others' words, thoughts, and actions and end up feeling bruised, wounded, and battered.

These include beliefs, behaviors, choices, sense of responsibility, and your ability to be intimate with others.

Examples of emotional and intellectual boundary invasions are:

- Not knowing how to separate your feelings from your partner's and allowing his/her mood to dictate your level of happiness or sadness (a.k.a. codependency).
- Sacrificing your plans, dreams, and goals in order to please others.

- Not taking responsibility for yourself and blaming others for your problems.

It seems obvious that no one would want his/her boundaries violated. So why do we allow it? Why do we NOT enforce or uphold our boundaries?

- FEAR of rejection and, ultimately, abandonment.

- FEAR of confrontation.

- GUILT.

- We were not taught healthy boundaries.

- We do not know how to build healthy boundaries.

Awareness is the first step in establishing and enforcing your boundaries. Assess the current state of your boundaries, using the list below:

HEALTHY BOUNDARIES allow you to:

- Have high self-esteem and self-respect.

- Share personal information gradually, in a mutually sharing and trusting relationship.

- Protect physical and emotional space from intrusion.

- Have an equal partnership where responsibility and power are shared.

- Be assertive. Confidently and truthfully say "yes" or "no" and be okay when others say "no" to you.

- Separate your needs, thoughts, feelings, and desires from others. Recognize that your boundaries and needs are different from others.

- Empower yourself to make healthy choices and take responsibility for yourself.

UNHEALTHY BOUNDARIES are characterized by:

- Sharing too much too soon or, at the other end of the spectrum, closing yourself off and not expressing your need and wants.

- Feeling responsible for others' happiness.

- Inability to say "no" for fear of rejection or abandonment.

- Weak sense of your own identity. You base how you feel about yourself on how others treat you.

- Disempowerment. You allow others to make decisions for you; consequently, you feel powerless and do not take responsibility for your own life.

Tips for Setting Healthy Boundaries

The following tips are modified from the book *Boundaries: Where You End and I Begin*, by Anne Katherine.

- When you identify the need to set a boundary, do it clearly, calmly, firmly, respectfully, and in as few words as possible. Do not justify, get angry, or apologize for the boundary you are setting.

- You are not responsible for the other person's reaction to the boundary you are setting. You are only responsible for communicating your boundary in a respectful manner. If it upset them, know it is their problem. Some people, especially those accustomed to controlling, abusing, or manipulating you, might test you. Plan on it, expect it, but remain firm. Remember, your behavior must match the boundaries you are setting. You cannot successfully establish a clear boundary if you send mixed messages by apologizing.

- At first, you will probably feel selfish, guilty, or embarrassed when you set a boundary. Do it anyway and tell yourself you have a right to self-care. Setting boundaries takes practice and determination.

Don't let anxiety or low self-esteem prevent you from taking care of yourself.

- When you feel anger or resentment or find yourself whining or complaining, you probably need to set a boundary. Listen to yourself, determine what you need to do or say, then communicate assertively.

- Learning to set healthy boundaries takes time. It is a process. Set them in your own time frame, not when someone else tells you to.

- Develop a support system of people who respect your right to set boundaries. Eliminate toxic persons from your life—those who want to manipulate, abuse, and control you.

Establishing healthy boundaries and enforcing them allows you to step into your authentic self with confidence. No one can like, love, or respect you if they don't authentically know you. And you deserve to be authentically liked, loved, and respected.

Living in the "Here and Now"

Keep your thoughts focused on the "here and now." Stay focused on the present. Fill your mind with thoughts and conversation related to "today and this week." Keep all your conversations in the present and future.

Resist Picking at Your Wound

Resist the temptation to think about or pick at your wound (Inner-Child), as he/she is healing, particularly when your mind and emotions are recovering and adjusting to living in the present. As your emotional wound continues to heal and the emotional skin re-forms, it is natural to experience emotional itching and irritation. You can easily aggravate your wound by talking or ruminating about the past injustice. It is vital that you allow the injury to heal by its own accord, as picking at it even at this later stage can still introduce new infections such as anger or bitterness. It can even lead to permanent scarring – depression, anxiety or addiction.

STEP 5

Nurturing the Emotions

Now that your wounds are well protected, we do not want to leave it malnourished, fragile and insignificant. At this point of the process you will learn the following central self-care components to keep your emotions healthy, vibrant and resilient:

1. 10 Rules for Emotional Health
2. Apply PETs (Positive Energizing Thoughts)
3. ANTs (Automatic Negative Thoughts) that Infest Human Minds
4. Changing Simple ANTs to PETs
5. Assertiveness Communication Skills
6. 10 Attitudes that Keep You from Expressing Your Feelings
7. 10 Attitudes that Prevent You from Listening
8. 5 Secrets of Effective Communication

Goal: Become an expert in maintaining your emotional health and wellness in tip-top shape.

10 Rules for Emotional Health

1) Take care of yourself. Take time to relax, exercise, eat well, spend time with people you enjoy and do activities that you find pleasurable. When you are the best you can be, you can be the best you can be in relationships.

2) Choose to find the positive in life experiences instead of focusing on the negatives. Most dark clouds have a silver lining and offer

opportunities for personal understanding and growth. When you accept that things are difficult and just do what you need to do, then it doesn't seem so difficult.

3) Let go of the past. If you can't change it and you have no control over it then let it go. Don't waste your energy on things that cannot benefit you. Forgive yourself and others.

4) Be respectful and responsible. Don't worry about the other people; do what you know is right for you. When you take ownership of your stuff, you feel good. Don't get caught up in blaming others.

5) Acknowledge and take credit for your successes and accomplishments. Avoid false modesty.

6) Take the time to develop one or two close friendships in which you can be honest about your thoughts and feelings.

7) Talk positively to yourself. We talk to ourselves all day long. If we are saying negative and fearful things then that is the way we feel.

8) Remove yourself from hurtful or damaging situations. Temporarily walk away from a situation that is getting out of control. Give yourself some space and problem solve a positive approach to dealing with it.

9) Accept that life is about choices and it is always bringing change to you to which requires adjustment.

10) Have a plan for the future. Develop long-term goals for yourself, but work on them one day at a time.

Apply PETs - Positive Energizing Thoughts

The mind is one of the hardest things to get under control and keep under control. Moment-by-moment thoughts play a critical role. We entertain ANTs (automatic negative thoughts) and PETs (positive energizing thoughts) on a daily basis (Amen, 2006).

Although we are capable of thinking reasonably about upsetting events, sometimes our ANTs are distorted or unreasonably negative. Distorted ANTs occur so rapidly that we hardly notice them, let alone stop to question them. Yet these ANTs instantaneously affect every part of your life including your thoughts, mood, sense of worth and behavior (Schiraldi, 2001).

Whenever you have a disappointed, angry or depressive thought, your brain releases chemicals that make your body feel tense. Likewise, positive thoughts release chemicals that make your whole body feel good, happy and alive.

In any life situation, two people can experience it in different ways based upon their thoughts. We can choose to think negatively or rationally. See the following situation.

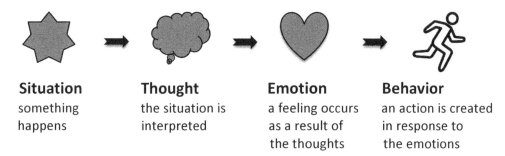

Situation
something
happens

Thought
the situation is
interpreted

Emotion
a feeling occurs
as a result of
the thoughts

Behavior
an action is created
in response to
the emotions

Situation: Jim and Jenny both receive a negative evaluation at work.

Jim

Negative Thought: "I can't do anything right at work. I bet I will get reprimanded for this!"

Emotion: Anxious, Afraid

Behavior: Jim takes the next day off work. He feels scared and avoids his boss. He is waiting to be punished.

Jenny

Rational Thought: "I guess I didn't work hard enough. I'll have to come up with a better plan for next time".

Emotions: Disappointed but motivated.

Behavior: Jenny seeks out her boss to talk about how she can improve. She approaches her next task as a challenge and gradually improves.

Is your mind infested with ANTs or is your mind filled with your favorite PETs? ANTs can invade your mind at any time. In order to rid yourself of these pests, you must monitor your thinking patterns; notice when they occur, identify them as false, and immediately talk back to them. Here are examples of ANTs that infest our lives…

ANTs that Infest Human Minds:

All-or-Nothing Thinking: With all or nothing thinking you hold yourself to the impossible standard of perfection. For example, "I have to do things perfectly because anything less is a failure"; "If I'm not performing perfectly, I'm a loser". This type of thinking is unreasonable because such absolute, black and white extremes rarely exist.

Disqualifying the Positives: You only see the bad in a situation. Dwelling on the negative overlooks the positive aspects. You disregard positives and so support your low self-esteem. "Nothing goes my way. I don't like my life. It feels like one disappointment after another." A variation is being overly judgmental: "Things aren't like they used to be. The world is falling apart. People aren't nice any more. I don't like what I see around me."

Negative Self-Labeling: You give yourself or someone else a negative label or name. "I'm a failure. If people knew the real me, they wouldn't like me. I am stupid." Such statements are unkind and inaccurate. We are to confine labels to behaviours. For example, a more precise statement: "I might not succeed in everything, but that doesn't mean I'm a failure."

Catastrophizing or Fortune Telling: Catastrophizing or fortune telling is to view or talk about an event or situation as worse than it actually is. It is predicting the worst possible outcome to a situation. For example: "If something is going to happen, it'll probably be the wort-case scenario." Asking the following questions will challenge the belief that something will be a catastrophe:

> ✓   What is the worst-case scenario?
> ✓   How likely could this happen on a scale of 0-10?
> ✓   If the worst happens, what will I do? (Thinking about a problem and working on an action plan will increase your sense of confidence).

Mind Reading: You believe that you know what another person is thinking even though they have not told you. "I can tell people don't like me because of the way they behave towards me."

Should Statements or Guilt Beating: You are thinking in words like, "should, must, ought, or have to." 'Should' statements are demands that you make of yourself or of other people. For example: "People should be fair"; "I should have known better"; "I must not make a mistake." Although these statements may sound motivating – they are not. It implies that "I should be so and so, and I'm not that way." This can trigger feelings of inadequacy, frustration, shame, and hopelessness.

One solution is to replace "should" with "would" or "could". For example: "It would be nice if I made the honor roll. I wonder how I could make the honor roll."

Overgeneralizing: Overgeneralizing is when you are thinking in words like always, all, never, no one, everyone, every time, everything. For example: "I *always* make mistakes"; "You *never* listen to my needs"; "*No one* listens to me"; "*Everyone* talks behind my back."

The antidote is to use more accurate statements: "*At times* I make mistakes"; "*Sometimes*, my co-worker doesn't listen to me"; "*Some* people talk behind my back."

Personalizing: You see yourself as more involved in negative events than you really are. For example, your friend blames you for not caring and you conclude, "It's all my fault. If I was nice we wouldn't have problems." You take full responsibility for the other person's anger, irritations and issues.

The alternative: Sometimes we can influence other peoples' decisions, but the final decision is theirs, not yours. You take responsibility for your part and let the other person take responsibility for their part.

Blaming: You blame someone else for the problems you have. Blaming is the opposite of personalizing. Whereas personalizing puts all the responsibility on yourself for your difficulties, blaming puts it all on something outside of yourself. For example: "You make me angry"; "My spouse ruined my life."

The problem with blaming is that you become the victim; too powerless to handle the situation. You are to acknowledge the outside influence, and take responsibility for your own well-being. "Yes, her behavior was unfair, but I don't have to turn bitter."

Making Feelings Facts: You translate your feelings into facts. For example: "I feel you don't want me – I'm not wanted"; "I feel alone - That must mean that you don't care about me." Feelings result from your thoughts. If your thoughts are inaccurate (as they often are when one is stressed or depressed), then your feelings may not reflect reality. Always remind yourself that feelings are not facts. When your thoughts become more realistic, your feelings become clearer.

Changing Simple ANTs to PETs

Exercise 1: Record Simple ANTs and Spoken Statements

One of the best ways to get rid of these ANTs is to write them down. For the next 7 days, keep an inventory of all the ANTs and spoken statements you compose. Twice a day, (noon and evening) spend 15 minutes recording every negative thought and statement you entertained. Using the ANTs and PETs LOG, record the ANTs and spoken word statements in the left column.

Keep an **ANTs and PETs LOG** similar to the following example:

ANTs – Automatic Negative Thoughts and Spoken Statements	PETs - Positive Energizing Thoughts and Spoken Statements
It's all my fault.	We both made mistakes, even though we did our best.
I always ruin everything.	Some things I do well, other things I need to improve.

Exercise 2: Translate ANTs and Spoken Statements in the right column.

Using the ANTs and PETs LOG on the previous page, begin translating the ANTs and spoken word statements to positive energizing thought and spoken word statements. Translate each statement on your list. Make sure that the PETs and spoken word statements are truly positive.

If you have trouble with the translation and are not completely sure that the PETs and spoken word statements are truly positive, ask for help. Ask a family member, friend, spouse, partner, colleague or therapist to help you with the translation part. Furthermore, ask a person to proof read the PETs and spoken word statements and verify their authenticity.

Example:

> **ANT:** "I'm not as good as other people."
> **PET:** "I'm a good person with many great qualities."

Exercise 3: Memorize PETs and Spoken Statements

For the next 21 days re-read and practice every PETs and spoken word statement. Twice a day (noon and evening), spend 10 minutes memorizing the list of positive statements, and practice your positive language all day long. As you become more fluent with the language, the positive spoken statements will develop into automatic PETs. Continue to practice the positive language until it becomes second nature.

Changing Complicated ANTs and Entangled Feelings to PETs

When you are highly stressed, anxious, angry or depressed, thoughts and feelings can swirl in your mind and become overwhelming. Putting your thoughts down on paper helps you sort out and see things more clearly. Remember that chaotic feelings result from your bewildering thoughts.

Before you start the **Thought/Feeling Record Worksheet** become familiar with the following 2 lists on the next page. Later, you'll want to memorize the emotions. You will be using them all the time.

1. **Unpleasant or** *Negative* **Feelings**
2. **Pleasant or** *Positive* **Feelings**

Unpleasant or *Negative* Feelings:

- **Anger:** irritated, insulting, annoyed, upset, bitter, aggressive, resentful, provoked, enraged, hostile, worked up, fuming, offensive.

- **Depressed:** discouraged, ashamed, miserable, disgusted, lousy, bad, guilty powerless, despicable, terrible, detestable, lousy, disappointed.

- **Confused:** upset, doubtful, uncertain, perplexed, sceptical, unsure, shy distrustful, embarrassed, hesitant, unbelieving, lost, tense.

- **Helpless:** alone, paralyzed, useless, empty, vulnerable, distressed, dominated, incapable, fatigued, inferior, forced, hesitant, despair.

- **Indifference:** insensitive, neutral, reserved, weary, bored, disinterested.

- **Afraid:** fearful, terrified, suspicious, anxious, panic, nervous, scared, worried, alarmed, timid, restless, frightened, doubtful, scared.

- **Hurt:** tormented, pained, rejected, injured, aching, victimized, alienated.

- **Sad:** tearful, sorrowful, pained, grief, anguish, unhappy, lonely, pessimistic.

Pleasant or *Positive* Feelings:

- **Open:** confident, accepting, free, sympathetic, interested, satisfied, kind, reliable, understanding, easy, amazed, receptive.

- **Happy:** joyous, thankful, satisfied, glad, important, delighted, fortunate.

- **Alive:** playful, energetic, courageous, optimistic, liberated, free, blessed, wonderful.

- **Good:** calm, peaceful, comfortable, pleased, relaxed, encouraged.

- **Love:** considerate, affectionate, sensitive, tender, devoted, sympathy, close, empathy.

- **Interested:** concerned, affected, intrigued, inquisitive, curious, fascinated, absorbed, nosy, snoopy, engrossed.

- **Positive:** eager, earnest, determined, bold, brave, optimistic, confident, keen, anxious, inspired, excited, enthusiastic, daring, challenging.

- **Strong:** free, sure, certain, unique, dynamic, secure, impulsive, and tenacious, rebellious, hardy.

Thought/Feeling Record Worksheet

Use the Thought/Feeling Record Worksheet for complex thought distortions and entangled feelings. There are 10 steps to the thought/feeling record. The first six steps will help you identify the automatic negative thoughts and the unpleasant feelings, and better understand where they came from. The next four steps will help you develop positive energizing thoughts, which in turn will produce pleasant feelings.

Write about unpleasant experiences that you would like to have handled differently. You can write about past or current negative events or behaviours. Start with easy ones first. Get a lot of practice before you deal with highly complicated experiences.

Understand Your ANTs (Automatic Negative Thoughts)

1. The situation: Briefly describe the situation that led to your unpleasant feelings. This will help you remember it later if you want to go back and study your notes.

"I made a mistake at work".

---

2. Initial thought: What thought first popped into your head? This was probably a subconscious or automatic thought that you have had before.

"I feel like a failure. If people knew the real me, they wouldn't like me".

---

3. Negative thinking and feelings: Identify the negative thinking and unpleasant feelings behind your initial thought. Choose one or more from the list of common types of negative thinking and list all your unpleasant feelings.

This is self-labelling and disqualifying the positives. It produces unpleasant feelings, sadness, fear, rejection, anger, jealousy, anxiety, stress, frustration, etc.

Automatic Negative Thoughts:

_____

_____

_____

Unpleasant Feelings

_____

_____

4. Source of negative belief: Is there a deep belief or fear driving this thinking? Can you trace your thinking back to a situation or person? Search your heart.

"I can hear the voice of my parent saying that I'm a failure and that I'll never amount to anything".

_____

_____

5. Challenge your thinking: Look at the evidence (both for and against it). Make sure you see the whole picture.

Evidence for: "I'm hard on myself. I don't always succeed. It's when I try to be perfect that I feel overwhelmed and disappointed in myself."

_____

_____

Evidence against: "I've had many successes. People have complimented me on my work. My friends see me as a good, honest, caring person."

_____

_____

_____

6. Consider the consequences: What are both the short-term and long-term consequences if you continue to think like this? Look at the physical, psychological, professional, emotional, and spiritual consequences.

"I'm damaging my self-esteem. If I continue to think like this, my negativity will affect my relationships and possibly my health. I'll become an exhausted, fearful, angry, sad, distrustful, insecure, doubtful, anxious, lonely, victimized and negative person".

_____

_____

Develop PETs (Positive Energizing Thoughts)

7. Alternative thinking: Once you've considered the facts, write down a healthier way of thinking. The previous steps of the thought/feeling record helped you understand your thinking and feelings. Now that you have let down your defences, you will be more open to alternative thinking and experience more pleasant feelings.

"I don't have to succeed at everything. I might not succeed at this, but that doesn't mean I fail at everything. I want to get rid of this negative thinking. I'm not gaining anything by being hard on myself."

_____

_____

_____

_____

8. Positive belief and affirmation: Write down a statement(s) that reflects your healthier beliefs (PETs). Find something that you can repeat to yourself.

"I am successful in many ways."

_____

_____

_____

9. Action plan: What action can you take to support your new thinking?

"I'm going to celebrate my victories and focus on the positives. The next time I slip (make a mistake), I won't dwell on the negatives and waste my energy. Instead, I'll focus on what I can learn from my slip."

_____

_____

_____

_____

10. Follow your improvement. Do you feel slightly better or more optimistic? This step reinforces the idea that if you change your thinking, you will change your mood. Gradually over time, your thinking, feelings and life will begin to change.

This is self-labelling and qualifying the positives. Your positive thinking continues to produce pleasant feelings: happy, playful, relaxed, loving, confident, secure, optimistic, etc.

List pleasant feelings you will experience over time:

_____

_____

Put PETs into your
emotional bank account.

The more you invest – the richer you feel/become.

Assertive Communication Skills

Communicating with others is a skill – but not necessarily a skill we are born with! Of course, some people are natural-born communicators, but most of us are not. But even if you were not born a communicator, do not despair – there is still hope. Fortunately for us, communicating honestly, openly and directly is a skill we can all learn. When connecting with self and others, learning to be assertive is a key factor. Before we take a look at the idea of assertiveness, we need to highlight important characteristics of bad communication and the rules of politeness.

Characteristics of Bad Communication

Truth: You insist that you are "right" and the other person is "wrong".

Blame: You say that the problem is the other person's fault.

Martyrdom: You claim that you're an innocent victim.

Put-Down: You imply that the other person is a loser because she/he "always" or "never" does certain things.

Hopelessness: You give up and insist there's no point in trying.

Demandingness: You say you're entitled to better treatment but you refuse to ask for what you want in a direct, straightforward way.

Denial: You insist that you don't feel angry/ hurt/sad when you really do.

Passive-Aggression: You pout, withdraw, say nothing, slam doors, storm out of rooms.

Self-Blame: Instead of dealing with the problem, you act as if you're an awful person.

Helping: Instead of hearing how sad, hurt or angry the other person feels, you try to "solve the problem" or "help" him/her.

Sarcasm: Your words or tone of voice convey tension or hostility, which you aren't openly acknowledging.

Scapegoating: You suggest that the other person has "a problem" and that you're sane, happy, and uninvolved in the conflict.

Defensiveness: You refuse to admit any wrongdoing or imperfection.

Counter-Attack: Instead of acknowledging how the other person feels, you respond to their criticism by criticizing them.

Diversion: Instead of dealing with how you both feel in the here-and-now, you list grievances about past injustices.

The Rules of Politeness:

The Do's	The Don'ts
Give sincere and positive appreciation. If you have an issue to resolve, sit down and discuss it in a constructive manner to manage your differences.	Don't complain or nag.
Be courteous and considerate.	Don't be selfish.
Express interest in the activities of others. Try to listen and ask questions.	Don't hog the conversation.
Give others a chance to finish speaking.	Don't suddenly interrupt.
Speak honestly and in a caring way.	Don't put others down.
Critique your ideas, but don't criticize yourself.	Don't put yourself down.
Focus on the present situation. If you have an issue, sit down and discuss some constructive solutions.	Don't bring up old resentments.
Think of the needs and wants of others. Be empathic. If you have an issue to resolve, sit down and work out a constructive solution.	Don't think only of your own needs and wants.
Be sensitive to others as you choose topics to discuss.	Don't embarrass or humiliate others.

Assertiveness Communication

Assertiveness means to communicate your thoughts and feelings honestly and appropriately. Assertiveness communication can be verbal and nonverbal. To express yourself assertively requires self-awareness and knowing what you want and need. It means showing yourself the same respect that you demonstrate toward others. Assertiveness generally helps you to develop self-respect, self-worth, and gain the respect of others. It also increases your chances for honest relationships, can help you to feel better about yourself and enhances your self-control in everyday situations. This in turn helps improve your decision-making skills and chances of getting what you really want from life.

If you do not assert yourself by letting other people know what your thoughts, feelings, wants, and needs are, then they are forced to make assumptions about you in those areas. Assumptions have about a 50% chance of being correct. That means you only have half a chance of people understanding you and responding to you in a way that you desire.

Once you begin to assert yourself, you will find that you will feel better about yourself, have more self-confidence, that you get more of what you want out of life, and that others will respect you more.

Be prepared that not everyone will be supportive of your changes in thinking and behavior. Some people that you interact with, such as family members or a significant other, may even demonstrate some negativity toward these changes. This could be because change is difficult for them to accept, they are comfortable with what is familiar to them, they benefitted from your passive, people-pleasing behavior, or they fear losing you through change.

However, you can't give up who you are to please other people, or to keep certain people in your life. Take one day at a time, focus on the positives, and be the best that you can be. If you explain as best you can and give them time to adjust to your new behavior, you may be pleasantly surprised when they come to respect you for your newfound directness and honesty.

To clarify the variations of responses and styles of communication and behavior, review the following descriptions. Identify the style(s) that you most often use. If you identify with categories 1-4, you want to make changes and learn category 5 - assertive communication.

1. **Passive**: Always giving into what others want. Don't want to make waves. Don't express your thoughts or feelings. You are afraid to say "no". Discounting your own wants and needs.

2. **Aggressive**: Being demanding, hostile, or rude. Insensitive to the rights of others. Intimidate others into doing what you want. Is disrespectful.

3. **Passive-Aggressive**: You tell people what they want to hear which avoids conflict. However, you really feel angry inside and you don't follow through on the expectations or requests, which results in the other person feeling frustrated, angry, confused, or resentful.

4. **Manipulative**: Attempt to get what you want by making others feel guilty. Tend to play the role of the victim or the martyr in order to get other people to take responsibility for taking care of your needs.

5. **Assertiveness**: Directly, honestly, and appropriately stating what your thoughts, feelings, needs, or wants are. You take responsibility for yourself and are respectful to others. You are an effective listener and problem solver.

In order to understand the difference between assertive communication and aggressive or passive communication, see table below:

Passive Communication	Assertive Communication	Aggressive Communication
Flight	Balance Point	Fight
Run Away	Your Own Power	Attack
Give Away Your Power	Stay in Your Power	Take Other's Power
Violate Your Own Limits	Mind Your Own	Violate the Limits of Others
Criticize Yourself	Take Responsibility for Yourself	Criticize Others
Make Yourself Wrong	Stand up for Your Rights	Make Others Wrong
Point the Finger at Yourself	Self-Power	Point the Finger at Others

The table shows that there is a balance point between the extremes of passive and aggressive communication – and this balance is assertive communication.

When you are passive, you implode and run away from conflict. You do not express your feelings or let others know what you want. The results are that others remain unaware of your feelings or wants, and they cannot be blamed for not responding to them. It also includes feeling guilty or as if you are imposing yourself, when you do attempt to ask for what you want. If you are not expressing your feelings, then others will tend to overlook them.

Being assertive is not the same as being aggressive. This is a very important distinction so I will repeat it. Assertiveness is not the same as aggression. Some people get the wrong idea and think assertiveness is aggression, but it's not. Aggression is self-enhancing behaviour at the expense of others. Being assertive is the opposite and translates into the ability to take care of oneself without violating the rights of other people.

Aggressiveness means that you express your rights but at the expense, degradation or humiliation of others. You are emotionally or physically forceful that the rights of others are not allowed to surface. You will often find that others become angry or resentful and lose respect for you. You put others on the defensive, leading them to withdraw or fight back rather than co-operate.

Aggressive behavior translates into demanding, abrasive or even hostile communication. Aggressive people are typically insensitive to the feelings, needs and rights of others and they attempt to get what they want through coercion or intimidation.

Many people are also passive-aggressive. Instead of openly confronting an issue, passive-aggressive people express angry, aggressive feelings in a covert way through what is called passive resistance.

Manipulative communication is where you try to get what you want by making others feel sorry for you. Instead of taking responsibility for meeting your own needs, you play the role of victim or martyr in order to get others to take care of you. If this does not work, you may become openly angry or indifferent. Manipulation only works as long as others fail to recognize what is happening. The person manipulated may feel confused or "crazy" at first; afterward they become angry and resentful toward the manipulator.

Assertive behavior involves asking for what you want or saying "no" to what you do not want in a simple, direct fashion that does not negate, attack or manipulates anyone else. Others feel comfortable when you are assertive, because they know where you stand and respect you for your honesty and forthrightness.

The Assertiveness Questionnaire

Exercise: An important step in assertiveness training is to identify those situations in which you want to be more assertive. Put a check mark in column "A" by the items that are applicable to you and then rate those items in column "B".

A = mark if item applies to you
B = rate degree of discomfort (1-5):

1. Comfortable
2. Mildly uncomfortable
3. Moderately uncomfortable
4. Very uncomfortable
5. Unbearably threatening

When do you behave non-assertively?

A	B	
__	__	asking for help
__	__	stating a difference of opinion
__	__	receiving and expressing negative feelings
__	__	dealing with someone who refuses to cooperate
__	__	speaking up about something that annoys you
__	__	talking when all eyes are on you
__	__	protesting being taken advantage of
__	__	saying "no"
__	__	responding to undeserved criticism
__	__	making requests of authority figures
__	__	negotiating for something you want
__	__	having to take charge
__	__	asking for cooperation
__	__	proposing an idea
__	__	taking charge
__	__	asking questions
__	__	dealing with attempts to make you feel guilty
__	__	asking for service
__	__	asking for a date or appointment
__	__	asking for favors
__	__	other _____

Who are the people with whom you are non-assertive?

A   B

A	B	
__	__	parents
__	__	co-workers
__	__	strangers
__	__	close friends
__	__	spouse or partner
__	__	employer
__	__	relatives
__	__	children
__	__	acquaintances
__	__	sales people, clerks, service people
__	__	more than two or three people in a group
__	__	authority figures
__	__	classmates
__	__	other _____

What do you want that you have been unable to achieve with non-assertive styles?

A   B

A	B	
__	__	approval for things you have done well
__	__	get help with certain tasks
__	__	more attention or time
__	__	be listened to and understood
__	__	make boring or frustrating situations more satisfying
__	__	not have to be nice all the time
__	__	confidence in speaking up when something is important
__	__	greater comfort with strangers, store clerks, etc.
__	__	get a new job, ask for interviews, raises, and so on
__	__	comfort with people who supervise you, or work under you
__	__	not feel angry and bitter a lot of the time
__	__	initiate satisfying sexual experiences
__	__	do something totally different and novel
__	__	have time by yourself
__	__	do things that are fun or relaxing for you
__	__	other _____

Exercise: Evaluating Your Responses

Examine your answers, and analyze them for an overall picture of what situations and people threaten you. How does non-assertive behavior contribute to the specific items you checked on the "what" list? In constructing your own assertiveness program, initially it will be useful to focus on items you rated as falling in the 2-3 range. These are the situations that you will find easiest to change. Items that are very uncomfortable or threatening can be tackled later.

Understand Your Feelings, Needs and Wants

To act assertively, you must be mindful of your feelings, needs and wants. It is difficult to be assertive unless you are clear about what it is you are feeling and what it is you want or do not want.

10 Attitudes that Keep You from Expressing Your Feelings

Conflict Phobia. You are afraid of conflicts and expressed feelings of anger. You may believe that people with good relationships shouldn't fight or argue. You may also believe that the people you care about will get hurt and would not be able handle it if you told them how you felt or what was truly on your mind. This is the "ostrich phenomenon" – you bury your head in the sand instead of dealing with problems.

Emotional Perfectionism. You believe that you shouldn't have irrational feelings like anger, jealousy, depression or anxiety. You think you should always be rational and in control of your emotions. You are afraid of being exposed as weak and vulnerable. You believe that people will look down on you if they find out how you really feel.

Fear of Disapproval and Rejection. You'd rather swallow your feelings and put up with some abuse than take the chance of making anyone mad at you. You feel an excessive need to please people and to meet everybody's expectations. You are afraid that people would not like you if you expressed your own ideas and feelings.

Passive-Aggressiveness. You give others the silent treatment by holding your hurt and anger inside and try to make them feel guilty instead of sharing your feelings.

Hopelessness. You feel convinced that your relationship cannot improve no matter what you do, so you give up. You may feel that you've already tried everything and nothing works. You may believe that your spouse is just too stubborn and insensitive to be able to change.

Low Self-Esteem. You believe that you are not entitled to express your feelings or to ask others for what you want but should always please others and meet their expectations.

Spontaneity. You believe that you have the right to say precisely what you think and feel when you are upset.

Mind Reading. You believe that people know what you feel and what you want without your having to express yourself directly. This gives you a perfect excuse to hold your feelings inside and to feel resentful because people don't seem to care.

Martyrdom. You are afraid to admit that you're angry because you don't want to give anyone the satisfaction of knowing they've upset you. You take enormous pride in controlling your emotions and suffering silently.

Need to solve problems. When you have a conflict with someone, you go around and around in circles to solve the problem instead of sharing your feelings openly and hearing how the other person feels.

It is important to become aware of what you are feeling and to become responsible for your own feelings. Often when a feeling is identified, your perception of a situation changes.

Understanding your feelings, needs and wants involves saying how you feel and saying directly what changes you would like to see happen. For example:

"I am feeling upset right now and I would like you to listen to me."

If you are feeling confused about your wants or needs, take your time to clarify them first by thinking about them, writing them down or talking about them with supportive others. Writing out a problem situation and formulating the details of how you will handle it can be very helpful. This trial run in writing can allow you to feel more prepared and confident when you actually confront the situation in real time.

You could also use role-play with a supportive friend to ask for what you want in advance. Be absolutely sure not to assume that others will know what you want. You have to make your needs known, because other people are not mind readers.

Be sure to specify the **"who," "when," "what," "how," the "fear,"** and the **"goal."** For example:

> *My friend Joan **(who)**, when we meet for coffee after work **(when)**, often goes on non-stop about her marriage problems **(what)**. I just sit there and try to be interested **(how)**. If I interrupt her, I'm afraid she'll think I just don't care **(fear)**. I'd like to be able to change the subject and talk sometimes about my own life **(goal)**.*

Furthermore, communication is one of the most powerful factors influencing the quality of a relationship; whether it is in a partnership, parent-child relationship or in a work situation.

Family background has a great influence on the ways we learned to communicate in early childhood. Although these may have been compatible with our own family's style, our patterns change as we grow and mature. However, some patterns may consciously or unconsciously influence the way we communicate in our present relationship and may not be compatible with those of our partner.

For example, if your family expressed negative feelings frequently and loudly, you may assume that this is the way to talk things out and you may resent your partner's unwillingness to argue. However, their attitude may also have been influenced by differing family patterns.

Listening skills are essential to good communication and must be developed and practiced. The goal of a good listener is not only to hear the words spoken, but also the feelings behind the words.

Before we take a look at developing better listening skills, we want to highlight 10 attitudes that prevent you from listening...

10 Attitudes that Prevent You from Listening

> **Truth.** You believe that you are right and the other person is wrong. You are preoccupied with proving your point instead of expressing your angry feelings more directly or trying to grasp how the other person is thinking and feeling.

Blame. You believe that the problem is the other person's fault. You feel overwhelmingly convinced that you're completely innocent and tell yourself that you have every right to blame the other person.

Need to be a Victim. You feel sorry for yourself and think that other people are treating you unfairly because of their insensitivity and selfishness. Your stubborn unwillingness to do anything assertive to make the situation better gives people the impression that you like the role of a martyr.

Self-Deception. You cannot imagine that you contribute to a problem because you cannot see the impact of your behavior on others. For example, you may complain that your spouse is dogmatic and stubborn and unwilling to listen, but you don't notice that you constantly contradict everything s/he tries to say.

Defensiveness. You are so fearful of criticism that you can't stand to hear anything negative or disagreeable. Instead of listening and trying to find some truth in the other person's point of view, you have the urge to argue and defend yourself.

Coercion Sensitivity. You are afraid of giving in or being bossed around. Other people seem controlling and domineering, and you feel that you must resist them.

Demandingness. You feel entitled to better treatment from others, and you get frustrated when they do not treat you as you expected. Instead of trying to understand what really motivates them, you insist that they are being unreasonable and have no right to feel and act the way they do.

Selfishness. You want what you want when you want it, and you throw a tantrum if you don't get it. You are not especially interested in what others may be thinking and feeling.

Mistrust. You put up a wall because you believe you will be taken advantage of if you listen and try to grasp what the other person is thinking and feeling.

Help Addiction. You feel the need to help people when all they want is to be listened to. When friends/family complain about how bad they feel, you make "helpful" suggestions and tell them what to do.

To listen effectively, you must be totally present to the other person, focusing your attention on what is being said, rather than on other distractions such as television, the newspaper, the children's behavior, or an idea you are waiting to express. In listening, you try to identify the theme or central message of your partner's words.

When we communicate, there is a high probability that the message we intend to convey will not be received exactly as we wish. What is really meant may not be said. When we talk to each other, the person listening automatically processes the message in terms of his or her own beliefs, values, goals and experience. Because we bring our own perceptions to any situation, misunderstandings frequently occur.

Conflict develops when one partner's behavior does not match the other partner's expectations, and poor communication sustains the conflict.

When conflict occurs, it often tends to be repeated and so it is important to learn to deal with it effectively.

Mutual respect is of high importance since the attitude of one or both partners is often at the heart of the issue, rather than being the issue itself. In a relationship with mutual respect, each partner seeks to understand and respect the other's point of view.

Pinpointing the real issue behind the conflict is also important. It often is identified as one of control, resentment, lack of respect or feelings of hurt and the need to retaliate. Once the issue has been identified, alternative ways to behave can be discussed and new agreements reached concerning the surface issue.

Seeking new areas of agreement is the next step followed by mutual decision-making. When both partners mutually participate in conflict resolution, they can develop creative agreements that are acceptable to both and are shared equally; cooperation replacing resistance.

Open dialogue is vital to a good relationship. Conflict is inevitable between two human beings who have different histories, different experiences and look at the world from different perspectives.

The ongoing process of blending two personalities into a relationship that is mutually enriching involves effort and pain. **To avoid this effort and pain is to avoid real intimacy and growth.** It is important to recognize that conflict is inevitable and to be prepared to deal with it in a positive manner.

Learning to Say No

An important part of being assertive is your ability to **say no** to requests that you do not want to meet. Saying no means that you **set limits on other people's demands** for your time and energy when such demands conflict with your own needs and wants. It also means that you can do this without feeling guilty.

In some cases, especially if you are dealing with someone with whom you do not want to promote a relationship, just saying: "*No thank you*" or "*No, I am not interested*" in a **firm, polite manner** should suffice.

If you need to make your statement stronger and more empathetic, you want to:

1) Look the person directly in the eyes
2) Raise the level of your voice slightly, and
3) Assert your position: "*I said no thank you.*"

In many other instances with acquaintances, friends and family, you may want to give the other person some explanation for turning down their request.

For example:

> "*I understand that you would really like to get together tonight* (acknowledge the person's request). *It turns out I have had a really long day and I feel exhausted* (explain your reasoning), *so I need to pass on tonight* (saying no). *Would there be another night later this week when we could get together?*" (alternative option).

In the end, learning to be assertive will enable you to obtain more of **what you want** and it will help **minimize frustration** and **resentment** in your relationships with partners, colleagues, family and friends. It will also help you to take more risks and to **ask more of life** in general, which will add to your **sense of autonomy** and **self-confidence**. Becoming assertive does, however, **take practice**. When you first attempt to act assertively with family and friends, be prepared to feel awkward. Also, be prepared for them not to understand what you are doing and possibly to even take offence. If you explain as best you can and give them time to adjust to your new behavior, you may be pleasantly surprised when they come to respect you for your new-found **directness and honestly**.

5 Secrets of Effective Communication

LISTENING SKILLS

1. **The Disarming Technique**. You find some truth in what the other person is saying, even if you feel convinced that what they're saying is totally wrong, unreasonable, irrational, or unfair.

2. **Empathy.** You put yourself in the other person's shoes and try to see the world through his or her eyes.

    a) **Thought empathy**: You paraphrase the other person's words.
    b) **Feeling empathy**: You acknowledge how they're probably feeling, given what they are saying to you.

3. **Inquiry:** You ask gentle, probing questions to learn more about what the other person is thinking and feeling.

SELF-EXPRESSION SKILLS

4. **"I FEEL" statements.** You express your feelings with "I feel" statements such as, "I feel upset" rather than with "you" statements such as, "You're wrong!" or "You're making me furious!"

    In expressing feelings, always be sure to own your reactions rather than blame them on someone else. The best way to do this is to speak about them in the first person, i.e.:

    "... I felt sad when you forgot to call at the time you said you would ..."

    First person statements acknowledge your responsibility for your feelings while second person statements generally accuse or judge. For example, instead of saying,

    "... you make me angry when you don't hear what I say ..."

    You can say, *"... I feel angry when you don't listen to me ..."*

5. **Stroking:** You find something genuinely positive to say to the other person, even in the heat of battle. This indicates that you respect the other person, even though you may be angry at each other.

Listening Skill #1: **The Disarming Technique**

1. Find some truth in what the other person says. They have to be right to some extent, since no one is ever 100 percent wrong. Usually, when you agree with the other person they will then stop arguing and agree with you! This remarkable phenomenon is called "The Law of Opposites."

2. If you feel angry or attacked, express your feelings with non-challenging "I feel" statements, such as *"I feel upset that . . ."* Avoid the temptation to argue or strike back. Don't get defensive.

3. Answer in such a way that your dignity and self-esteem are maintained, even if you agree with the other person's criticism.

4. Give up your desire to lash out or blame the other person. Try to maintain an attitude of mutual respect so that nobody has to lose face or feel put down.

5. Avoid getting into who is "right" or "wrong." This serves no purpose!

Listening Skill #2: **Empathy**

1. Put yourself in the other person's shoes. Listen carefully and try to understand accurately what they are thinking as they are talking. State what you think the other person is thinking by saying something like *"It sounds like..."* and then paraphrase respectfully what you understood them to say.

2. Also try to understand what the other person is feeling. Listen with your "third ear." Notice their body language. Do they appear tense? Angry? Hurt? Acknowledge what the person is feeling, based on what they said and the manner in which they said it.

3. Ask a question to confirm how they are feeling, such as *"I can imagine you must be feeling frustrated with me. Is this true?"* Ask them if you have accurately understood what they are thinking and feeling.

4. Use an "I feel" statement to let them know how you would feel if you were in their shoes. You might say, "*I would be feeling the same way if this had happened to me.*"

5. Accept the other person's feelings. Do not be hostile, critical, or defensive. Let them know that you are willing to hear what they have to say.

Listening Skill #3: **Inquiry**

1. Most people have an intense fear of expressing their feelings openly. They are always afraid of conflict and will avoid telling you they're angry with you. They deny their feelings, and then act them out. You can prevent this if you ask the other person to tell you more about their negative feelings.

2. You can also ask the other person to tell you more about the specific problem that makes them feel upset. What are the details? How often does it happen? How do they feel about it? What did you do that turned them off?

3. Ask the person to tell you directly what you did or said that hurt their feelings. When they tell you, don't get defensive. Instead, use empathy and the disarming technique. Find some truth in what they have to say. If you feel upset or irritated or put down, express your feelings with an "I feel" statement.

4. Use a tone of voice that is respectful, not challenging, when asking what made them unhappy or angry. Do not use any form of sarcasm.

5. Don't be afraid of anger and conflict. They are healthy. Don't let the other person's unhappy feelings go unexpressed. That makes the feelings much more intense.

Self-Expression Skill #4: **"I feel" Statements**

1. When expressing your feelings, use "I feel" statements, such as "I **feel upset.**" "I have told you twice that I am not interested in your product and you are still trying to sell it to me. **I am starting to**

feel really irritated." Avoid "you" statements, such as "You're making me upset."

These "you" statements sound critical and judgmental and always trigger fights and arguments! Here are some examples:

- *You always ...*
- *You never ...*
- *You are wrong ...*
- *It's your fault ...*
- *You shouldn't ...*
- *You're making me angry ...*

2. **Don't act out your feelings!** State them!

   Use "**I feel**" statements. Acting out emotions can take the form of:

   - Pouting
   - Being sarcastic
   - Being critical
   - Door slamming
   - Stone silence
   - Being rude
   - Drinking too much
   - Negative body language

3. **Unpleasant feelings** can be expressed by saying:

   "**I feel ...**" with words like: "**I feel concerned** ..."

   - *I feel pressured*
   - *I feel cohorts*
   - *I feel frustrated*
   - *I feel angry*
   - *I feel Stressed*
   - *I feel misunderstood*
   - *I feel abused*
   - *I feel uncomfortable*

4. **Vulnerable feelings** can be expressed by saying,

   "**I feel ...**" with words like: "**rejected ...**"

   - *I feel rejected*
   - *I feel hurt*
   - *I feel sad*
   - *I feel disappointed*
   - *I feel intimidated*
   - *I feel unloved*
   - *I feel fear*
   - *I feel offended*

5. **Wishes and desires** can be expressed by saying something like:

   *"**I would like** to spend more time with you."*
   *"**I really want** us to work out this problem and to be closer."*
   *"**I would appreciate it if** you call me to let me know you're going to be late."*
   *"**I want you** to try to understand my point of view."*

Self-Expression Skill #5: **Stroking**

1. Generally speaking, most people want to feel cared for and appreciated. The greatest fear that people have is being put down, rejected, or judged.

2. Reassure the other person by clearly letting them know that you respect them and that they are important to you, even if you are angry or disagreeing with them at the moment.

3. Let the other person know that you want to work out the problem in a mutually satisfactory way.

4. Don't criticize or condemn them as a person. Nothing is ever gained by doing this. Attacking them personally is very different from commenting negatively on something they are doing or thinking.

5. The listening and self-expression skills are only techniques. Real communication results from the spirit of genuine respect for yourself and for the other person. If your goal is to prove yourself right, to blame the other person, or to get back at them, any communication technique will fail. But if your goal is to resolve the problem and to understand how the other person is thinking and feeling, these powerful methods will help you resolve conflicts and enjoy greater intimacy.

STEP 6

Loving Your Inner-Child

As seen earlier in the workbook, our Inner-Child lives within all of us, he or she is the part of us that feels emotions and is playful, intuitive and creative. Usually hidden under our grown-up personas, the Inner-Child holds the key to increasing our mental, emotional, and social well-being.

No matter how hopeless or helpless you currently feel, these strategies can help boost your intimacy in relationships, recovery from addictions, and increase the creativity and wisdom of your inner self.

Next, you will learn to take your Inner-Child seriously, and to consciously communicate with your little girl or boy within; to listen to how he or she feels and what he or she needs from you. Your Inner-Child's needs of love, acceptance, protection, nurturance, and understanding remain the same today as when you were a child. As adults, we ineffectively try to force others into fulfilling our Inner-Child's needs for us. But this never works.

Authentic adulthood requires both accepting our painful past and taking full responsibility for taking care of our Inner-Child's needs; for being a "good enough" parent to him or her now and in the future. If you are a woman, no matter how self-reliant you are, your little girl, who is very tender, needs your help. If you are a man, no matter how macho you are, you have a little boy inside who craves warmth and affection.

You will learn to relate to your Inner-Child exactly as a good parent relates to a flesh-and-blood child; providing unconditional love, discipline, limits, boundaries, coaching, forgiveness, protection and structure. These are all—along with support, nurturance, and acceptance—indispensable elements of loving and living with any child, whether metaphorical or actual. Initiating and maintaining an ongoing dialogue between the two can reach acceptance, authenticity, commitment, loyalty, and unconditional love between your Inner-Child and mature Adult-Self. A new, mutually beneficial, cooperative, symbiotic relationship can be created in which the sometimes-conflicting needs of both your Adult-Self and Inner-Child can be creatively satisfied.

Love is the greatest healing power I know. Love can heal even the deepest and most painful memories because love brings the light of understanding to the dark corners of your mind. No matter how painful your early childhood was, loving your Inner-Child now will help continue the healing process. In the privacy of your own mind, you can make new choices and think new thoughts. Thoughts of forgiveness and love for your Inner-Child will open pathways and God will support you in your efforts.

Note: *You may call God by a different name. Keep addressing God with the name that you are accustomed.*

It is important to remember that this is a process and will not get done all at once. You need to learn how to parent your Inner-Child. He or she will teach you what is needed as time goes on. You will need to be as patient with your boy or girl as if you had adopted a real child with a troubled background.

Learn to love yourself – Adult-Self and Inner-Child - in the same way as you would like to be loved by others. Be supportive, encouraging, forgiving, kind and patient with your Adult-Self and your Inner-Child. Do not be rude, self-seeking, easily angered, envious, proud or delighting in wrongs.

Bonding Techniques

- Value and validate his or her feelings.
- Let your body express the love you have for your boy or girl by holding a pillow or stuffed animal, rocking, humming, stroking, doing anything you do to comfort an actual child.
- Start doing things that your girl or boy would love to do.

- Treat each other the way you would like to be treated. Trust your instincts on this. Let your girl or boy tell you what feels good to her or him.

- Do not let any critical voices tell you that it is silly to rock and hum a lullaby. It is not silly—it is valuable practice in loving yourself.

- Protect, support, guide, coach, teach and love each other.

- Let this best friendship mature into becoming the greatest gift that life can offer.

You will need to do this practice over and over as your Inner-Child gradually learns to trust you. Over time you will learn to be the caring parent that your Inner-Child never had. You will share your future with the wonderful, free, and loving spirit that is your Inner-Child.

If you are struggling with getting to know you Inner-Child, try the following: Find a picture of yourself at the age of 5 or 6 and try to get a sense of who this little boy or girl was. Let your mind and emotions relax as you look at yourself in the picture.

Learning to love is not always easy. Your desire to love must be stronger than your desire to protect yourself against the pain of rejection, loneliness, grief, or whatever else you fear. Love is more important than anything else, even being controlled, hurt or manipulated.

Bridging Aids to Help You Open Up

If you are struggling to open up to show love toward yourself and others, you want to develop bridges. A bridge will act as an aid to help you open your heart.

Generosity: A fast way to open a closed heart is to ask yourself: "What can I give to myself and others freely?" As you ask the question, your heart opens up to love. For example, if you are going to a party, instead of worrying about, "How can I get people to like me?" ask yourself, "What can I give?" You can give people a smile, your interests, your acceptance, etc. The moment you decide to give, your heart opens and your spirit fills you with love and peace.

God: Ask God to help you open your heart. God's love is abundant, unconditional and always here for you when you ask for help. Often, the problem is that the wounded self does not believe that anything in the unseen spiritual realm is for them. Until you are willing to take a "leap of faith" and open your heart, you will not know God.

If you do not believe in prayers, then try the following bridges to help open your heart to learn about love:

- Doing volunteer work.
- Reading emotional and spiritual literature.
- Journaling your thoughts, feelings and inner voice.
- Letting yourself cry.
- Listening to or playing music.
- Attending a 12 Step program or other support group meetings.
- Playing with a child or a pet.
- Allowing yourself to be held by a loving person.
- Talking openly with a friend.

Compassion: Your Inner-Child will not open up if you are shaming and being judgmental of his or her feelings or behaviors. If you approach an actual child and ask, "What are you feeling?" in a condemning tone, the child will not feel safe in giving you an honest answer. If you ask the question in a compassionate tone, the child will probably open up and tell you. The same is true for your Inner-Child.

Compassionately Dialogue with Your Inner-Child

You want to learn to open your arms to all of you – strengths, deficits, quirks and uniqueness. Welcome everything that comes up within you, do not judge or condemn areas that are unpleasant at the present time. Ask your Inner-Child to tell you how she or he feels. Allow your Inner-Child to be authentic and embrace all his or her feelings – pleasant and unpleasant. Ask your Inner-Child questions such as:

- "What am I telling you or doing that is making you feel anxious (angry, depressed, shamed, judged, etc.)?"
- "Am I loving you?"

- "How do you feel when I give you alcohol (drugs, junk food, money, etc.) whenever you are feeling hurt, lonely, bored, angry, anxious or fearful?"

- "What do you really need from me when you are feeling stressed, hurt, angry, frustrated, bad?"

- "Do I make you feel safe?"

- "Am I your best friend?"

Remember that no feelings are ever wrong or bad. They either feel pleasant or unpleasant. Feelings are a reservoir of information that you need. Your job is to discover the information. You want to understand with love, compassion and curiosity, not only your feelings, but also your thoughts, behaviors and memories.

For some people, using a doll or stuffed animal acting as a "surrogate Inner-Child" can help start the dialogue. Hold a doll or stuffed animal while you are asking your Inner-Child questions. You may want to hug your stuffed animal to comfort your Inner-Child. For others, the best way to start the dialogue is to verbalize or write the conversation. For example:

Adult: What am I telling you or doing that is making you feel anxious?

Child: You are telling me that I clam up in social settings. When others notice this, they will think that I have problems.

Adult: Yes, I have been telling you that. How do you feel when I tell you this?

Child: I feel pressured, and worry that I will make a fool of myself. I worry that people will not like me or view me as weird.

Adult: I can see why you would feel anxious. I say this a lot, and I always thought my anxiety was coming from other people. I'm the one who is causing it. What do you really need from me when you are feeling anxious in a social setting?

Child: I need you to be mindful of my anxieties. Accept them; hold me and gently talk to me. You can help me find ways to relax or look for positive things to do.

You can have a dialogue any time. Whatever you are feeling or is happening in your life, keep yourself in good company. Explore your gifts, passions and talents, what brings you joy, what is your true calling, what fulfills your soul.

Note: The adult always asks the child feeling questions; "What are you feeling?" The child always asks the adult thinking questions; "What are you thinking?"

Listen to Your Inner-Child

After you asked the questions, listen to your Inner-Child. The answer will come from deep within you, not from your head. When you listen to your Inner-Child, you will be able to find out what you really need. You might ask, "What is it you are really seeking or feeling hungry for?" The wounded, immature child will want a short-term fix – new clothes, food, sex, alcohol or illicit drugs. By compassionately embracing and listening to your feelings, you can discover what your Inner-Child really wants and needs.

Once you allow your Inner-Child to voice his or her feelings, you will discover that your Inner-Child is in need of unconditional love and connection. He or she is looking to you, the Adult-Self, for comfort, understanding, acceptance, protection and caring.

For some of you, if you notice that you are not getting anywhere with your dialogue, see if you are taking full responsibility for your feelings, and engage your Inner-Child with compassion. You may be asking all the right questions, but make sure your tone is gentle, not condemning or embarrassing.

If your Inner-Child does not want to talk to you, no worries. Keep working on your loving Adult-Self. Once you provide consistent emotional safety, he or she will come out of hiding and open up to you.

A Spiritual Perspective

If you continue to lack connection with your Inner-Child, try to connect with God. The following story illustrates an amazing connection between an adult and her Inner-Child (Klugger 2010):

"I asked Judy to connect to her [God] with her hand on her heart and ask [God] to fill her with love and compassion so that she could open up to the young girl in the photos. Next, Judy stared into the eyes of the girl in the photos for a very long time. Then closing her eyes, she imagined picking up this girl and holding her very close to her heart. After just a few minutes Judy was able to describe how sweet, helpful, shy, and loving this little girl was. All she wanted was to be loved and accepted by the people in her life. At that point, Judy asked [God] to fill her with love so that she could bring that love to her "little girl". It became an amazing breakthrough for Judy. She was now able to really relate to this part of herself, her essence. Over the next few weeks Judy worked diligently to get to know her Inner-Child on a deeper level. Through the Inner Bonding process and lots of dialogue, she learned what "little Judy's'" favourite color was, that she truly loved music and dance. That she adored walking in nature or skipping stones along the riverbed on sunny afternoons. Judy began to discover many things that brought that part of her true joy. She realized what a great honour and a privilege it was to know and love her "little girl". In knowing this she began taking the loving action by giving her "little girl" the gifts of doing the things she loved to do. There were outings in the park, singing to a tune she loved, and sometimes dancing to a song she found moving. Taking the loving action for her Inner-Child felt wonderful and in turn was instrumental in further developing Judy's loving adult. She now feels deeply connected to her essence and feels tremendous love, understanding and compassion for that part of her. With the Inner Bonding process, Judy is now able to bring from [God] the love and acceptance to and through her that she always wanted to have and to share."

STEP 7

Loving God

In Ezekiel 36:26-27, the Lord says, "I will put my Spirit within you and cause you to walk in my ways." It is amazing to realize God's Spirit lives within us and often we don't pay any attention to Him at all.

I Corinthians 3:16 says, "Do you not know your body is a temple of the Holy Spirit." Andrew Murray, in his book *The Spirit of Christ*, elaborated on this in a way that was very helpful to me. He said in the Jewish temple there were three courts: the outer court, the inner court, and the Holy of holies.

Murray described how our physical bodies symbolize the outer court. The inner court is made up of our mind, our will and our emotions. The Holy of holies represents our spirit where God dwells. The three courts of our temple characterize our physical body, mind/emotions and spirit.

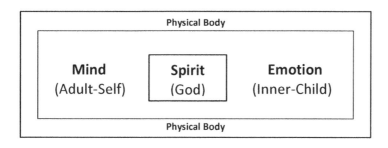

Physical Body		
Mind (Adult-Self)	**Spirit** (God)	**Emotion** (Inner-Child)
Physical Body		

How to Love God

You can love God by giving your life to God. In order to love God with your whole heart, you must give your whole heart and your whole life to God.

This does not mean that you cannot love anyone else. It is just the opposite. God loves all people. The more you love God, the more you will truly love your Adult-Self, your Inner-Child, your friends, your family, your coworkers and everyone else you encounter.

But more specifically, giving your life to God means you can have a personal relationship with Him. God loves you and wants to be your best friend, protector and coach.

How will this happen? You can receive Christ right now. Remember that Jesus says, "I'm standing at the door and I'm knocking. If anyone hears my voice and opens the door, I will come in." (Revelations 3:20). Would you like to respond to his invitation? Here is how.

The precise words you use to commit yourself to God are not important. He knows the intentions of your heart. If you are unsure of what to say, this might help you put it into words:

> "Jesus, I would like to start a relationship with You. I realize that I have avoided You all my life, similar to how I avoided my Inner-Child. Without my Inner-Child, and You, I now realize what's been missing from my life. I also understand that I need You to clean my heart so that we can start up anew. Forgive me for all my wrongs (sins) and I ask You to join my Inner-Child and I. We place our trust in You and we thank You for forgiving us. Thank You for accepting our friendship. We are excited about growing in this new relationship with You. Help us to grow our friendship. We want us to become best of friends. Thank you".

If you sincerely asked Jesus into your life, if you asked Him to become your friend, then He has just come into your life. Now, you are starting a personal relationship with God.

Congratulations! You have just made the most important decision of your life – asking Jesus into your life. Becoming a friend of Jesus is an exciting, life-transforming first step in your journey with God.

Dialogue with God

How does God communicate, and to whom?

God communicates to everyone - all the time. The question is not to whom does he talk, but who listens? Maybe the reason most of us feel like we cannot hear God is we are too busy talking. It is so tempting to ask God to say what we want Him to say instead of just focusing on what He is already and how it applies in our lives.

God can communicate in a variety of ways, including through the Bible, prayer, or other believers, whom God uses to encourage us and help us understand His will. He wants to speak to us. He wants us to get it right. God's Word is His will. He has given us the Bible as a tool to better know and understand who He is and what His plans are for each of us.

While it is possible for God to speak to someone in an audible voice, it's typically "a deep inner conviction about God's will."

God does not communicate with words alone. His most common communication is through deep feelings and convictions. Feelings is the language of the soul. If you want to know what is true for you about something, look to how you are feeling about it. Feelings and convictions are sometimes difficult to discover and often even more difficult to acknowledge. The truth is hidden in your deepest feelings and convictions.

God also communicates with thought. Thought and feelings are not the same, although they can occur at the same time. In communicating with thought, he often uses images and pictures. For this reason, thoughts are more effective than mere words as tools of communication.

In addition to feelings, convictions and thoughts, God also uses the vehicle of experiences as a grand communicator.

You may ask: "How can I know this communication is from God? How do I know this is not my own imagination?" The challenge is one of discernment. The difficulty is knowing the difference between messages from God and data from other sources. God's voice is always your highest thought, your clearest word and your grandest feeling. Anything less is from another source.

The following guidelines will help you know the difference:

1) The highest thought is always that thought which contains joy.
2) The clearest words are those words that contain truth.
3) The grandest feeling is the feeling of love.

Joy, truth, and love are interchangeable, and one always leads to the other. It matters not in which order they are placed.

God also works through our imagination. He will bring you the exact right thoughts, words or feelings, at any given moment, suited precisely to the purpose at hand, using one device, or several.

Why do some people seem to hear more of God's communication than others? Because some people are willing to listen. They are willing to hear, and they are willing to remain open to the communication even when it seems scary, crazy, or downright wrong.

God loves to hear what you have to say when you talk with Him. But how often do you listen to what God has to say to you?

It's easy to fall into the habit of just talking to God, rather than trying to hear what God is telling you. It's always worthwhile, however, to make the effort to listen to God whenever you communicate with Him. A conversation is meant to be a two-way dialogue between you and God.

You can enjoy conversations with God when you read the Bible by asking God questions about the verses you are reading and then listening for God's responses in your mind. Start by asking God to quiet your mind so you will not be distracted, and to speak to you. Then read a passage from the Bible slowly, several times. Write down the thoughts that occur to you. Finally, read over what you have written to discern if God is speaking to you through those words, and if so, how you should respond to His message.

Building Your Ultimate Friendship

Friendship with one's self and God is all-important because without it, one cannot be friends with anyone else in the world.

We run around begging for love, attention and validation from everyone around us. We look for "special" people that will make us feel "special." We clutter our lives with all kind of glorious, expensive and precious things and the more stuff we accumulate, the less we seem to have and the emptier our lives seem to get.

Unless we build a friendship with God and ourselves, none of these things will bring us long lasting happiness… none of these things will make us feel whole and complete.

You are now part of a wonderful, diverse family – God, Adult-Self and Inner-Child - which I call "The Love Triangle". It is here where you experience true love; where your identity is built and where you feel at home.

The closer you get to God and your Self, and the stronger the love triangle you build, the easier life gets and the happier you become.

If you make friends with yourself and God you will never be alone. The degree of love I'm able to share with others depends solely on the degree of love I share between my Adult-Self, my Inner-Child and my Father-God.

Love Triangle

Spirit
(God)

Emotion   **Mind**
(Inner-Child)   (Adult-Self)

The following exercise is designed to help you build the friendship you have with your Adult-Self (mind), your Inner-Child (emotions) and your God (spirit), so that you can attract all the love, happiness and abundance that you so much desire.

How do three members of one body become best of friends?

With the same techniques you have used to build all of your other friendships.

Start by getting to know each other. Spend time together talking and listening, sharing ideas, thoughts and interests. Do stuff that is of interest to all three members, such as working, building diverse friendships and relationships, playing, travelling, praying, serving, exercising, reading the Bible, etc.

How do I talk or listen to my other members?

I found that the best and quickest way to get the three members together to converse is to have a written conversation. It is very difficult to achieve a relaxed and clear dialogue between the three members in your mind, without the facilitation of a written conversation.

Good communication can only occur when full attention is given to one conversation at a time. Do not try to accomplish this exercise solely in your mind. You will not be able to gain the full benefits of this exercise.

Exercise: Written Dialogue Process

First, schedule a time and location to meet. Second, record the dialogue. Third, relax and let your thoughts, emotions, and spirit flow freely during your conversation. Some people may become tongue-tied during the first meeting.

Once you have written several conversations, each dialogue becomes more natural and begins to unify with your daily activities and routines. Your dialogue will begin to feel more comforting, pleasing, exciting, enriching and enlightening.

To help you get started, I have included a sample of a written conversation between the Inner-Child (Johnny), Adult-Self (John) and Spirit (God). To include God in the conversation, use the Bible to help you 'hear' from God.

Sample of a Beginner's Dialogue:

John: How's my Johnny doing? Did you have a nice day?

Johnny: I had a great day. I'm starting to feel better about our friendship. I like the way you talk with me. You're no longer angry with others and me. And I like how we are becoming better friends with our Heavenly Father.

God: "Love is patient, love is kind.... It is not rude, it is not self-seeking, it is not easily angered, and it keeps no record of wrongs." *1 Corinthians 13:4a-5.*

Johnny: God is so right. Keep it up Dad. How was your day?

John: I had a great day. I got a lot done at work. And I am proud of you. In how you stayed patient and didn't complain about the extra assignment I had to finish at work. Thanks for understanding. I'll make up the lost time with you. You're a great son. I want to love you more and more.

Johnny: I love . . .. *(Continue the conversation here with your Inner-Child, Adult-Self and Spirit).*

Sample of an Advanced Dialogue:

John: Why are you drinking again? I'm sure there's a good reason. Is there some way I'm not taking care of you? I really want to know what the problem is.

Johnny: I feel anxious a lot. I'm drinking because I feel anxious and scared.

John: But what are you anxious about?

Johnny: I just want to make sure Alicia (spouse) is happy. She seems so happy when I'm with her, so I try to be with her a lot, and then I don't have time to do other things I want to do—or have to do. And I never have any time alone anymore.

John: Well, would you feel better if we spent more time alone?

Johnny: I don't know. I'm afraid that Alicia would not be happy and that scares me.

John: Are you saying that you feel responsible for Alicia's happiness?

Johnny: Yes. Aren't we together to make each other happy? Dad made sure that Mom never felt alone. He was always available for her. Mom would get angry if Dad wasn't there when she wanted him there.

John: And you believe Alicia is the same way?

Johnny: I don't know, but I'm afraid she is.

John: Do you want us to be with her like Dad was with Mom?

Johnny: I don't know. I just feel trapped. I love Alicia, but I hate not being able to do what I want to do.

John: It sounds like you are making Alicia's feelings and needs more important than ours. You're taking care of her Inner-Child instead of taking care of us, and it is making you very anxious. I can see that drinking gives us an excuse to have some time alone. I've given up some of the things that are important to us, like going to the gym, and I drink when you feel anxious about this. So, God, what would be more loving way to sooth Johnny's anxieties?

God: Plan time to go to the gym and have time alone - you have to plan it into your day just as you plan time to work and sleep and spend time with Alicia. If you don't plan it, it won't happen.

John: How do I deal with Johnny's anxiety if Alicia is sad or upset about my doing this? Do I have the right to take care of Johnny if she is upset?

God: Alicia's feelings are her own responsibility. Your well-being is your responsibility. You have the right and the responsibility to take good care of Johnny. You can be caring about Alicia, but let her handle her own inner child's feelings.

John: What do I do if she gets mad at me, or gets angry like Mom?

God: Take good care of Johnny's loving behaviour. Keep telling Johnny that you are being loving to him and to Alicia when you take care of us. You can talk with Alicia and explore the conflict with her, and both of you will learn a lot.

John: So, if I start to exercise again and take time alone for us and keep telling Johnny that this is loving to both him and Alicia, maybe I can get through this anxiety without drinking. And when she gets angry, I need to remind Johnny of all this - that I am being loving and that I'm not responsible for her feelings. She needs to work them out with her Inner-Child or I can offer to explore her feelings with her. Sounds good to me, but I guess I'll have to try it and see how it works.

God: Ask for My help and strength and I will give it to you. I will give you what you need.

Next Steps

The moment you trust in Jesus, you enter into an unbreakable relationship with God. You will never be the same - both now and for all eternity! God wants you to experience how much he loves you. He wants you to learn how to do life with him. Here are 5 steps:

1. **Talk to God about everything**. Tell him your innermost secrets. Whenever you are afraid or you are at a total loss – talk to him. This can be done in your mind, verbally or through a journal. He wants to know everything. He wants to help you with everything. He is a perfect friend. How awesome is that!

2. **Read his love letter – the Bible**. It is the food for your soul. It is your life roadmap and your life-building manual. Study his love letters, take notes, and practice the life skills and strategies.

3. **Become part of his bigger family**. There are millions of people that have the same relationship you have. You are a brother or sister in God's family. Find people in spiritual circles – spiritual life groups, church, mission organization, spiritual interest groups, recreational groups, etc.

4. **Do what makes God happy - stop what makes him sad**. This is the same in every healthy relationship, including your relationship with your Inner-Child. Ask God what he would like you to change and tell him that you need his help to create the change. You can hear his voice deep within your belly.

5. **Tell your friends about your most important love relationship**. Ask God to give you an opportunity to talk about your relationship. Ask God to open someone's heart and to give you the words to speak.

Unless you, the Adult-Self take new, loving action on your Inner-Child's behalf, nothing really changes and nothing heals. For example, if your son came to you and told you that he was worried about your anger, and you listened and understood but made no attempt to change your behaviors, your son would not feel heard. Likewise, if your Inner-Child is in need of your love, compassion, connection, healthy boundaries, a fit and healthy body or just plain fun, and you listen and understand but take no action, your Inner-Child will feel unloved, abandoned, saddened, wounded, upset or unhappy.

You can tell yourself the truth all day, you can stare into the mirror and affirm over and over that you are a beautiful, wonderful child of God, but if you do not treat yourself as a beautiful, wonderful child of God, your Inner-Child will not believe your affirmations. Words mean very little without action. A loving Adult-Self takes actions on behalf of his or her Inner-Child.

When you fail to take loving actions, do not be hard on yourself. For example, when you slip up and become overly angry, do not beat yourself up. Be understanding, forgive yourself and use the opportunity to practice your anger management skills. Give yourself permission and room to practice and develop your best friendship. You cannot learn a new behavior without spending hours practicing the skills.

Become a self-coach. Establish a coaching relationship between your Adult-Self and your Inner-Child. Likewise, allow God to be your coach. A coaching style will expect growth to transpire, encourage failures and falls, support tears, set discipline, celebrate victories, and display compassion.

Taking loving action means learning to love both the gifted and the wounded self. It means to accept and embrace all of you. It means to release the hurt, shamed, angry and frightened parts of you and embrace them with unconditional love and compassion.

Understand that your wounded self has been doing his or her best to take care of you and help you feel safe. Loving actions mean understanding and having compassion for all the parts of you that you have hated or judged as inadequate, unlovable and unworthy. You heal your false beliefs when you learn to be loving to your wounded self.

Here are some love actions you want to give yourself with the help of God:

- Become resistant to criticism and fears of rejection as you stop taking other people's behavior personally.
- Stop being controlled by others, as you learn to set loving boundaries.
- Learn assertive communication, and stop being aggressive or passive.
- Be open to caring, bonding and connecting, not withdrawing, and becoming angry, blaming or judging.
- Learn to become a loving parent, coach, and friend to your Inner-Child.
- Fully depend on God's guidance, grace and unconditional love.
- Face your pain in order to heal your wounded self.
- Look after your health and wellness – nutrition, exercise, meditation, and rest.
- Set a positive attitude and be thankful throughout the day.
- Focus on being gentle, kind, loving toward self and others.
- You treat yourself the way you would like to be treated by others.
- Stay in sync with your Inner-Child and God's presence all day long.

- Risk losing something (addiction, greed, resentment, loneliness, etc.) that has control over you in order to gain your true self, your freedom, your dreams, your passions and connection with God.

- Give yourself the same compassion, kindness and care that you would give to a good friend.

Self-Compassionate Assessment Tool

Once you have taken loving actions, you will need to evaluate whether the action is working for you.

Exercise: Please read each statement carefully before answering. To the left of each item, indicate how often you behave in the stated manner, using the following scale: (Pommier, Neff & Gucht, 2010).

Almost Never	Occasionally	About Half Of the Time	Fairly Often	Almost Always
1	2	3	4	5

1. I'm disapproving and judgmental about my own flaws and inadequacies.

2. When I'm feeling down I tend to obsess and fixate on everything that's wrong.

3. When something painful happens I try to take a balanced view of the situation.

4. I am intolerant and impatient towards those aspects of my personality I don't like.

5. When I fail at something important to me I become consumed by feelings of inadequacy.

6. When something upsets me I try to keep my emotions in balance.

7. I try to be understanding and patient towards those aspects of my personality I don't like.

_____ **8.** I try to see may failures as part of the human condition.

_____ **9.** When I feel inadequate in some way, I try to remind myself that most people share feelings of inadequacy.

_____ **10.** When I'm going through a very difficult time, I give myself the caring and tenderness I need.

_____ **11.** When I'm feeling down, I tend to feel that most other people are probably happier than I am.

_____ **12.** When I fail at something that's important to me, I tend to feel alone in my failure.

Healthy Self-Compassion

1. Add your answers for questions 3, 6, 7, 8, 9, 10. These are indicators of a healthy self-compassion.

My Score	Scoring Key
	Mindfulness Items: (question 3 + 6)
	Self-Kindness Items: (question 7 + 10)
	Common Humanity Items: (question 8 + 9)
Total	
	Degree of Healthy Self-Compassion

Healthy Self-Compassion Score Interpretations - will tell you how healthy your self-compaction is.

24-30	High degree of unhealthy self-compassion
18	Moderate degree of unhealthy self-compassion
6-12	Self-compassion is in the healthy range

Unhealthy Self-Compassion

2. Add your answers for questions 1, 2, 4, 5, 11, 12. These are indicators of an unhealthy self-compassion.

My Score	Scoring Key
	Over-Identified Items: (question 5 + 2)
	Self-Judgment Items: (question 1 + 4)
	Isolation Items: (question 11 + 12)
Total	
	Degree of Unhealthy Self-Compassion

Unhealthy Self-Compassion Score Interpretations - will tell you how unhealthy your self-compassion is.

24-30	High degree of healthy self-compassion
18	Moderate degree of healthy self-compassion
6-12	Self-compassion is in the unhealthy range

Practicing all 7 Steps

For most of you, this has been an extremely difficult and amazing healing journey. Your emotional wounds and injuries had a devastating impact on your life before the start of your recovery.

Today you're feeling so much better – better than you could have ever imagined. The emotional wounds that once hurt, depressed and scared you are healing. In time, they will be completely healed.

As the emotional wounds heal it is important to continue to integrate the seven steps outlined in this workbook. Having the knowledge alone is not enough. Continue to apply and practice these skills until they become second nature.

Once you learn to take responsibility for your own emotional wounds, feelings, thoughts, and actions and to nurture your "Adult-Self, Inner-Child, Sprit-God" relationship, your path is open to build your life dreams, passions, goals, and healthy relationships.

The power struggles that exist in so many relationships disappear as you learn to treat self and others with unconditional love. Life battles, emotional injuries, ANTs and conflicts get resolved in healthy ways when your life skills – emotional wound care, assertive communication, PETs and conflict resolution - are well developed. Your relationships will improve, whether or not your family, friends, or partner learn the skills. You will be well equipped to manage any type of emotional injury, ANT and conflict. In addition, you become an esteemed role model to your family, friends, coworkers, partner, community, and country.

You will start to experience genuine love and learn to appropriately meet all of your needs. More and more, you will experience a greater sense of fullness in your heart, a securer and safer inner confidence, and greater joy that will overflow from within your soul. Feelings of anger, bitterness, loneliness, sadness, fear, shame, guilt and insecurity will slowly be replaced with feelings of joy, peace, happiness, compassion, and freedom. Your negative self-worth, emptiness within and neglectful attitude that led you to addictive and destructive behavior will eventually disappear as you continue to nurture your bond with your Inner-Child and your Heavenly Father.

Steadily, your disconnection from self and others that has emotionally starved you will fade. As you nourish self and your Inner-Child with your spiritual companion's love, you will experience a sense of oneness. Instead of hurting yourself and others, you will start loving yourself and others. Once you become comfortable sharing love, you will feel a deep trust in yourself, others, and your Heavenly Father. You will no longer have to *struggle* to believe in yourself and God; you will get to *know* yourself and God in a more peaceful fashion.

As your love triangle matures, you will never have to wait for someone to fill your emptiness. You will never have to feel alone. You will have the complete freedom to fill yourself with love and peace whenever you want. You have complete freedom to take action for yourself.

And remember, allow yourself to be parented by your Heavenly Father. Let him meet your deepest inner needs. Likewise, parent your Inner-Child in the same way your Heavenly Father parents you. Share your Heavenly Father's gift of love with yourself, your neighbors and the world.

Summing Up

On our journey together, we have explored a variety of emotional wound self-care skills. As with any skills, emotional wound self-care skills take time to acquire and practice to maintain. In time, you will incorporate most of the skills such as letter writing, journaling, forgiveness and letting go without much effort. With other skills such as assertiveness communication, boundary setting and thinking PETs, you will need to set aside time for further practice.

When life bruises and injures you or you want to enhance your love triangle, remember to refer to this First Aid Kit and rehearse the skills that have meaning to you. If emotional bruises and injuries can heal once, they can heal again.

Like any other important health practice, nursing your emotional wounds is an ongoing process. Like other useful habits, once you become good at nursing your emotional wounds and maintaining a healthy mind, heart, spirit, and relationship, the life skills will become second nature.

To summarize and reinforce your most important skills, as well as to serve as a quick reminder during difficult times, please review the entire First Aid Kit, and list below those ideas and skills that you most want to practice and remember.

Ideas and Skills You Want to Practice and Remember:

Final Thoughts

I have elaborated on seven steps of healing your emotional wounds and creating a healthy you. For every person, the profile of the emotional wounding will be different, but the processes of healing and wellbeing will be the same.

Untreated emotional wounds will cause physical, mental, emotional and spiritual impairment. They can set off mental health disorders like depression, anxiety and addiction. They can wipe out relationships, add to job failures, obscure life purpose or direction, and ultimately destroy life.

Airing out the emotional wound, along with letting the injustice go, forgiving the person, acquiring appropriate life skills, and developing a vibrant "best-friend" – Adult-self, Inner-Child, Spirit-God partnership - will minimize the risk of further infection and maximize the healing process.

I invite you to continue to be a team player in the growth of your life so you can heal your past, build your present and shape your future. Give yourself full permission to love yourself, to be yourself and to trust yourself. Stay honest, forgive yourself and treat yourself in the way you would like to be treated. Continue to love your Inner-Child, to honor your God and to love others.

Living with scars does not mean you are disadvantaged or incomplete. As a matter of fact, healed wounds help craft character, self-confidence, emotional intelligence, spiritual maturity, honest relationships, contentment and "the real stuff" we all long to experience. Your healing has unlocked large reservoirs of fuel (new knowledge, love and wisdom), which will supply you with new wealth of strength to continue your work in becoming your very best.

I encourage you to share your cleansing, healing and empowering experience. Let others see how your hard work radically changed your life. Share this cleansing recipe with others. They too, will be able to experience the same level of emotional and spiritual freedom, and happiness you are beginning to enjoy.

Healing emotional wounds means healing families, marriages, relationships, communities and countries. Proper and early intervention can go a long way in decreasing many of the problems shared in this First Aid Kit. If required, I encourage you to seek counselling or life coaching to help you complete the entire cleansing program. And lastly, I would love to hear your story, your cleansing experience and your healing journey.

Bibliography

Amen, D. G. 2006. *ADD in Intimate Relationships: A Comprehensive Guide For Couples.* Newport Beach: MindWorks Press.

Katherine, Anne. 2000*. Boundaries: Where You End and I Begin.* New York: Touchstone Publishing.

Klugger, Deb. 2010. Learning to Love Your Inner Child. http://www.innerbonding.com/show-article/2645/learning-to-love-your-inner-child.html

Leman, K., and R. Carlson. 1989. *Unlocking the Secrets of Your Childhood Memories.* Nashville: Thomas Nelson.

Monbourquette, Jean. 2000. *How to Forgive: A Step-by-Step Guide.* Toronto: Novalis Publishing.

Raes, F., Pommier, E., Neff, K.D., and Gucht, D.V. 2010. "Construction and Factorial Validation of a Short Form of the Self-Compassion Scale." *Clinical Psychology and Psychotherapy 18*:255-255.

Schiraldi, R. Glenn. 2001. *The Self-Esteem Workbook,* Oakland: New Harbringer Publications, Inc.

Author's Bio

John Schurmann is the founder of Schurmann Counselling & Life Coaching (www.coachme.ca).

He is a registered clinical social worker; individual, couple and family psychotherapist; ADD specialist and life coach. He has worked closely with individuals, couples, families, groups and organizations for more than twenty years.

John holds three degrees including a master's degree in clinical social work from Wilfrid Laurier University. He has extensive training in specialized areas of counselling: marital and family therapy, mental health issues, child and adult ADD, psychiatry, spirituality, sexuality, family violence and alcohol/drug abuse.

His passion for emotional wound care started while writing his thesis; *Inner Healing: Freedom from Memories of the Past* (1990) in partial fulfillment of the requirements for the degree of Bachelor of Arts in Psychology at Trinity Western University, Langley, British Columbia, Canada.

Since his university years, John's passion in emotional health and wellness continued to evolve in his counselling practice. Not only has he helped to turn individuals, relationships and families around - equipping them with the skills and ability to make their lives healthier - he is an inspired instrument, helping people heal their emotional wounds.

It is said about John Schurmann; *"You are outstanding in helping me heal my emotional wounds, giving me new skills to handle my life events, giving me new hope, a new outlook and a sense of adventure. John got me back on track, helped me improve my emotional and spiritual life, marriage, relationship, work situation and believed in me in resolving my life issues."*

John has a full time counselling practice in Markham, Ontario, Canada. He is married to Rita and enjoys spending time with his sons, Matthew and Daniel. He loves to learn, travel, ski, spend time with his extended family and friends, and loves his relationship with God.

Made in the USA
Las Vegas, NV
27 November 2021

35424959R10070